AN OPEN MIND

John,

Best wishes,

Anthony.

AN OPEN MIND
THE WORK OF HUDSON ARCHITECTS

Artifice
books on architecture

TO MY DAD, WHO TAUGHT ME TO MAKE
SOMETHING OUT OF NOTHING.

TO JENNY, MY GREATEST SUPPORT
AND GREATEST CRITIC.

CONTENTS

PREFACE
ANTHONY HUDSON

Once, when frustrated over the direction a project was taking—thinking it was hopeless with nothing going for it—I told my father that I needed inspiration. In his typical farmer's way he immediately retorted: "Inspiration! Why does everyone want inspiration? Look here, all you need is to look at an ear of wheat, that's inspiration!" He meant, I believe, that none of my education and learning was particularly useful for the task in hand unless I looked at what was in front of my own eyes there and then. Being open to the creative possibilities in front of one's nose is the leitmotif of *An Open Mind*: the characteristics of a rural or urban landscape, the practical demands of construction, and a celebration of living needs. This approach avoids trying to impose an architectural solution, and instead encourages a design to grow from what is given in time and place while enriching it with experience and knowledge of the past.

The book tells the stories of 18 projects covering private houses and public buildings. They are stories of the commissioning, design and development of the projects as well as revealing more hidden qualities and layers of meaning that are less immediately evident. *An Open Mind* is not only intentionally rich in imagery but also focuses on detail with a selection of plans at the back of the book. Our thinking, though rooted in architectural history and drawing upon a wealth of references and cues from other contemporary and historical cultures and traditions, is ultimately about the site and its topography, the feel, form and materiality of the landscape (whether urban or rural) and a desire to tell a story with the building. Always evident is a meaningful and thoughtful celebration of the particularities of day-to-day living: in housing, the organisation of spaces as a frame for living and, in general, the creation of a particular architecture related to site and users. The practice has developed an approach to a contemporary vernacular which allows what is available to determine the direction of a project. As well as referring to local materials and construction techniques, this means working in ways that are determined by site conditions, available skills, tools and technology, or the needs of particular clients or users of the building.

An Open Mind explores these themes and is split into three chapters: "Dwelling", "Making" and "Sharing". A short essay by Peter Blundell Jones, Sarah Wigglesworth and Alan Powers precedes each. Jay Merrick's Introduction puts the work into context, explaining the influences extending from the exotic—including Indian and Islamic art and architecture—to the more familiar inspirations of a farming background, study at Cambridge and the Polytechnic of Central London, and working with the architect David Lea. He considers the practice's concerns for making a rich and evocative architecture that resonates with associations.

The projects in the first chapter, "Dwelling", demonstrate how our houses respond to a particular location and celebrate domestic living. In his essay Peter Blundell Jones focuses on the preoccupation with details of domestic architecture and the importance and value of the particular characteristics of a place. This interest in the site, orientation and the wider architectural context is analysed with reference to Arts and Crafts precedent, the spatial complexities of Adolf Loos' *Raumplan* and the modernist language of Le Corbusier. Further, Blundell Jones sets out the practice's interest in the symbolic deployment of certain architectural elements, such as the columns at Baggy House, and the ingenious use of devices such as the architectural promenade.

The second chapter, "Making", concerns the contingencies of the building process and making the most of what you have. Sarah Wigglesworth's essay places the work with reference to the idea of a vernacular architecture, suggesting that the projects are a provocative instance of a contemporary vernacular informed as much by 'making' and a resourcefulness informed by my background as by the practice's ability to use the most up-to-date building materials and technologies.

The final chapter, "Sharing", looks at living in the public world. In many ways it reflects the themes of the previous chapters in the celebration of living and inventive construction, but also focuses on how this can bring community benefit. Alan Powers discusses our work within the broader discourse of civic architecture and highlights the practice's interest in addressing architectural problems within an urban context. In more detail, Powers is concerned with the practice's work as informed by international references such as Robert Venturi's *Complexity and Contradiction in Architecture*, as well as an original interpretation of post-war English municipal architecture.

What I hope *An Open Mind* shows is a rich body of work that is considered and responsive: buildings and spaces based on simple ideas of need and comfort, the here and now and rooted in experience. And hopefully the results are eloquent spaces that, on different levels, are both complex and simple—and ultimately wonderful places for people to inhabit.

LAYERS OF MEANING

JAY MERRICK

Baggy House.

Be like a garland maker, O king, and not like a charcoal burner.

That exhortation comes from the 1,500 year old north Indian Hindu epic, *The Mahabharata*, and it is one of Anthony Hudson's touchstones. For him, the image does not require the supporting decor of maharishis and ashrams—though it does suggest the possibility of one of his seminal heroes, Adolf Loos, as the garlanded modernist equivalent of a self-liberating sadhu holy man. And yet, it is the image of the charcoal burner that gives the story of his architectural development its proper beginning. It is tempting to think of Anthony Hudson, and his work, as escapees from the glowing ashes of architectural dogma.

He studied architecture at Cambridge in the 1970s. "There was a consensus that the teachers had to agree a collective viewpoint", he recalls. "Architects like Lutyens were seen as retrograde—not didactic enough. At that point, Corb and Wright and the five points were preferred. I liked Lutyens, Voysey and Lethaby, so I found the situation quite soul-destroying."

"I remember being absolutely shocked to see the Villa Savoye. The colour and the references made me think of the villas at Pompeii. But we were taught nothing about the architectonic quality of the Villa Savoye, or its incredible plan. I found the Villa Savoye was not as it was taught. To me, it actually *reinforced* the idea of history—that a building should come from somewhere. It is what makes sense of Ronchamp, the richness of the thinking, the sources. And I was bowled over when I went to Prague. But Loos was never talked about. He was treated as a dry art-historical ornament of the Secession."

After taking his degree in 1977, he went to deepest Wales for two years to assist David Lea, one of Britain's seminal environmental architects who, in 2010, co-designed the widely praised Wales Institute for Sustainable Education. Hudson's stint with Lea was as much about ditch-digging and tree-planting as architecture, but Lea's huge commitment to vernacular architecture and the environment made a deep and indelible imprint. There followed a year in India, since when Hudson's devoted interest in that country has continued, and strengthened. "The Hindu religion", he notes, "is about experiencing the gods that personify different aspects of life, gods that make sense of life—an acceptance of diversity. There's none of the petty bourgeois conflict. There is a control of the ego."

Salvation Army.

Feering Bury Barn.

His experiences in Wales and India tempered him. Hudson is not didactic, either personally or architecturally. He radiates a sense of open enquiry, which is rooted in his fascination with expressive choreographies of materials, and subtle *roman a clef* architectural effects. "My practice's architecture is not minimalist, but it is modern", he says. "It's not reductive. I do think that there is some consistency both in the celebration of richness of form, treatment of materials, and their sensual enjoyment. I like to think it is inclusive and deals with the complexities of life. Ultimately, our architecture is about creating lovely places for people to inhabit."

There is no Hudson Architects design brand. Instead, his practice, based in Norwich, has designed and delivered a stream of buildings of exceptional formal range. Few practices, of any size, can have produced architecture of such striking material and compositional variety.

Three examples form a compelling triangulation of Hudson's architectural range: the physically and metaphorically complex Baggy House in Devon; the Venturiesque Salvation Army Citadel in Chelmsford, with elevations that suggest stage-flats and a verse from St John's gospel cut into one facade like a circuit-board; and the extraordinary assembly of found agricultural objects that has surely made Hudson's reinvention of the Grade II listed Feering Bury Barn in Essex the most interesting, and delightful, example of environmentally artful architecture since Wigglesworth and Till's Straw Bale House in 2001.

The point about found objects—and architectural ideas—is that they can only convey potent new meanings if they are encountered, and used, in a way that rejects previous associations and certainties. And it was Hudson's strong reaction against the charcoal burning certainties of architectural study in Cambridge, under the then new professorial leadership of Colin St John Wilson, that was crucial in turning him away from what he experienced as an architectural Puritanism founded on a prescribed pantheon of historic architectural masters, and on specific and constrained material palettes.

Hudson, from a Norfolk tenant farming family of considerable lineage, was always profoundly interested in history and old buildings, and admits that he only began to notice modern architecture in his late teenage years. At Cambridge, his instinct was "to go back to a different history, not this terrific falsity—elevations that told

Baggy House.

a lie, inside appearing on the outside, truth to materials. I was more interested in Venturi's book, *Complexity and Contradiction in Architecture*. His projects were of the vernacular, and complex rather than stripping things down."

On his return from India, Hudson applied to the Architectural Association, where "my incredibly dry portfolio" prompted his interviewer to say: "You've lost your sense of fun." He duly enrolled at the Polytechnic of Central London (now the University of Westminster) where he studied under Doug Clelland and Eric Parry. "Everything had changed", he recalls. "There were teaching studios. Everything was up for grabs architecturally—interesting, but terrifying. Everything was available. You could raid history. It was the start of the most critically dreadful PoMo. But Doug Clelland and Eric Parry had just finished their first building. And so my thought was: how do you pull this postmodern world together? I was very disappointed by the work I did. I can remember working on a project and doing it in the idiom of somebody else—Ungers. It wasn't authentic."

Hudson's teachers were going a step beyond purely architectonic appreciation. And he freely admits: "I found it incredibly difficult to work within that historical, iconographical material realm." In essence, then, Hudson largely rejected the PoMo and phenomenological tropes of architectural garland making. And other generative ideas, seeking a different kind of postmodernism, duly took their place.

Hudson's first fully realised statement of architectural intent came in 1994, with the completion of Baggy House, overlooking the sea in North Devon. Today, he feels that, in some ways, this building's signifiers and references are over-rich. But his approach was novel, and very ambitious. "The design was about a choreography of materials and form. Womb-like on its north-facing side. The hallway very low, the ceiling lead-clad, and the chimney supported on a granite dolmen monolith.

"There are hidden meanings. The design started as a central room, with four rooms off it. Everything on the ground floor is riven stone, then polished slate, then timber, then glass. It was the idea of the nomad versus the Wrightian cave man. Bedrooms with arched ceilings. Every detail had a *raison d'etre*, as Dalibor Vesely says. I've never done this so completely since then." Baggy House was the Royal Fine Art Commission and *Sunday Times* 1994 Building of the Year—a brilliant entrée for Hudson.

Pushpanjali.

Light House.

Feering Bury Barn.

"Loos' Villa Müller was critical in attempting Baggy House", he says. "It was the first time I realised that this kind of architecture could be done. Another building I love is the Medieval Strangers Hall Museum in Norwich, which is a wonderful jigsaw puzzle in 3-D. Why can't we have this richness in modern buildings?"

Even so, Hudson cites his early attempts at designing Baggy House as an example of over-richness: "Mackintosh chimney, Devon barn vernacular, main living space like the Teheran Palace viewing platform. Every room with a different level, and a different ceiling height. A complex section like a Chinese puzzle. After six months, I thought: this is shit, it is not going anywhere. I felt overwhelmed by the number of ideas I was trying to incorporate. And I felt very dissatisfied with how the first designs appeared. Too many intellectual things in the way, and not allowing the design to develop organically." Ultimately, however, all of Hudson's original ideas remained in the final design, pulled together in a more effective form.

In 2005, his design for a newbuild home and guest house in Pushpanjali, Delhi, produced a comparably ambitious architecture, whose assurance in plan and section produced engrossing connections between volumes, qualities of light, and atmospheres. A year later, Light House in Belper, Derbyshire, confirmed this shift towards a more physically and intellectually limber approach to design: the architectural layering here is expressed horizontally rather than vertically, the stone core of the house giving way, successively, and without forced compressions or decompressions, to timber and glass.

Today, this confident and measured expression of richness of design has become Hudson's *modus operandi*. "Feering Bury Barn, for example, is full of colour and texture, but not so heavily designed", he emphasises. "The whole thing has been stitched together with found pieces–no tension wires to show off the contrast of new and old. It is traditional–the way my father would have done it on his farm. I think that's what interests me. That question: with what I have got, what can I do? It's the Louis Kahn thing: what does this building want to be? You set the premise, and you get guided. It's less imposed, and more relaxed. That is the theory, anyhow!"

Hudson certainly seeks a richness of formal assembly, but he is equally intent on making sure that the making, joining, and tensions of architecture are revealed.

Salvation Army.

He cites Sergei Eisenstein's ideas about cinematic choreographies of colour and texture; the internal iconography of Gaugin's palette is another inspiration. He deplores the current pressures to invest architecture with overloaded imagery.

"The key challenge is getting a coherent form", he says. "A design must always start with how a building is going to be occupied. Pliny's Villa is an example—a place used at different times of the day, and in different seasons. The making of form is, for me, more and more about *discovering*. The less hard you think about it, and the more you think about how you would actually *make* it. And it is not until you do buildings, and can draw fluently, that you can think properly about architecture."

"You need to develop an understanding of the experience of a building. The Salvation Army Citadel in Chelmsford, for example. There was no point in having a complicated facade on the side of the building that was next to a dual-carriageway if you are seeing the facade as you go past at 80 kilometres per hour. In choosing a building's form and materials, it is absolutely crucial that you have the narratives —architecture as a story—coming through coherently."

Hudson is not averse to, as he puts it, "robbing and reassembling forms and details from favourite buildings and places". Buildings should offer layers of meaning—some aspects which everyone will see and enjoy, but also other more hidden qualities which are not at first noticed. The purpose of all this is to try and ensure that a design, despite its many facets, has consistency—that it isn't just robbing the past and treating history as valueless, like certain kinds of postmodern architecture do. It is, instead, about recreating a new but coherent environment.

And he emphasises a critically important point: "The narratives in my architecture are not abstract. They become unified. A work of architecture has to have depth. It needs to be worked through, and thought through—the idea, and the way you *make* the building. So, however complicated it is, there is a choreography of the building. I am interested in the specifics of things, the notion of the organic, and the hugely important question of context. There has to be a link between every architectural choice."

Feering Bury Barn.

These choices can never, of course, be effectively pursued in an isolated way, and Hudson has a remarkable ability to absorb his clients' aspirations, and then involve them in the development of design concepts. Indeed, in appropriate circumstances, he has no difficulty in allowing a client to 'personalise' design details, or even structural interventions, during construction.

At Feering Bury Barn, his clients, the artists Ben and Freddie Coode-Adams, organised their own sub-contractors for metalwork and woodwork. "It is a sixteenth century timber frame barn", says Hudson. "We were not trying to get to the mystic origins of the barn, as a building type. But we wanted to keep as many layers as possible." The 'found' 1970s concrete grain silos were already inside the barn, but were repositioned at one end. Metal silos were left where they were, outside the building and alongside it, and will ultimately be converted into bedrooms. 40 per cent of the barn's large roof is meshed rooflights, which from the outside, looks like corrugated iron.

"It was such a pleasure working with Ben", says Hudson. "What we were really thinking about was to use every single piece that had originally been taken out of the building—and not forcing something to be experienced as something it wasn't." Even in their new domesticity, the silos remain, quite unmistakably, silos.

Hudson's recomposition of objects at Feering Bury Barn, and the quality of their presence, is extraordinary: there is not the slightest sense of superficial eclecticism. "It is this almost Hindu way of looking at things", he suggests, "a notion of the true vernacular, the way you approach something within the confines of the project. That creates a story. And as soon as you take this approach, everything has a distinct relative importance. I'm more and more interested in that. It is incredibly liberating, architecturally."

And yet, ironically, it is Bavent House, surrounded by reed beds at Reydon in Suffolk, that seems most clearly to have embodied the precisely designed richness of space and detail that turned a potential charcoal burner architect into one of the profession's most interesting garland makers. The irony is that, externally, Bavent House could easily be taken for a classic 1970s Cantabrian design. There are three materials to be seen—iroko, zinc, and glass—and they clothe what seems, at first, to be a deliberately tough, pragmatic architectural form.

Bavent House.

Seen from the northwest, the zinc cowl that covers the northeastern elevation, and the long slanting eaves overhang along the northwestern face are rather brusque; but one deduces immediately that they were dictated by the directions of the prevailing winds. Hudson says the design was partially inspired by the tarred black fish sheds on the shingle beach at Southwold.

From the outside there is no hint about what lies in store internally—though one might have heeded a remark of Hudson's about the Villa Muller: "The interior responds to the particulars of the client. Every room has its own character, but they are tied together in a story." And at Reydon, on Rissemere Lane East, he has achieved something remarkably consonant with that idea.

The clients, Richard and Lucy Turvill, have always loved the Kettles Yard gallery in Cambridge, and particularly its loose-fit, slightly ad hoc feel. They took to Hudson's concept of a building that was conceptually like an egg—hard on the outside, but soft where it had been broken into. That certainly explains the raw toughness of the iroko and the zinc.

And yet, inside, this is an architecture of almost panoptic, Loosian qualities in which volumes and angles seem to segue effortlessly in an arrangement of individually characterful spaces. From the landing, one can count half a dozen angles formed by various surfaces coming together, and as many distinct modulations of light and shadow generated by the full-height central volume; the material details are characteristically deft. Unlike the early designs for Baggy House, there is no sense of "too many intellectual things in the way". Instead, one experiences a clearly expressed ensemble of spatial qualities, punctuated by material details with delightful sensual tractions.

Walking around this house with Anthony Hudson, one feels very far removed from the burning *ghats* of postmodern architectural excess, and closer to a much more intimately articulated architectural tableau; and nearer, too, to something very like what the visionary engineer, Cecil Balmond, calls the "generative line" of informal possibility. For Balmond, of course, that line is to do with the expressive potentials of algorithmic and number theory patterns in relation to structure and architecture.

Bavent House.

In Anthony Hudson's case, one can't help imagining a generative line that must have begun with the indestructible blue baling twine that he so fondly remembers his father using on the family farm; a line that became knotted and doubtful for a period, but which then unravelled interestingly—and just enough to produce an architectural choreographer of the found, the imagined and the made.

DWELLING

ARCHITECTURE, VIEW, AND THE VALUE OF PLACE
PETER BLUNDELL JONES

BAGGY HOUSE

BAGGY POOL

LIGHT HOUSE

DROP HOUSE

PUSHPANJALI

BAVENT HOUSE

The different living spaces at Baggy House overlap, providing a rich backdrop for comfortable modern living. The kitchen at the centre with, clockwise from bottom right, breakfast table, steps up to the dining room and down to the family room, living room balcony and glass stairs to the guest rooms.

ARCHITECTURE, VIEW, AND THE VALUE OF PLACE

PETER BLUNDELL JONES

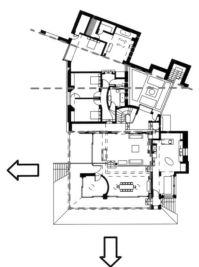

Baggy House.

What is the value of a view? Estate agents have great difficulty in deciding how much it adds to a house, but have to admit a greater proportion when it overlooks sea or lake, and hotel owners know all too well the increased rate for the room with the view over that overlooking the back yard. Proof positive that a view can matter was given by Roger Ulrich's famous hospital study comparing identical rooms in which patients recovered from operations, one with a view and the other not.[1] He found that those with the view went home on average a day earlier: a huge economic saving. If there is a good view it needs a good window to frame it, a terrace to sit and contemplate it, or even a crow's nest. Give the view equally to all rooms in the house and it is negated by repetition, even impossible to escape. Good architecture can control just how a view is presented and discovered, where it is revealed or denied, how it is contrasted with another or made part of a narrative journey. This is especially important in modern houses intended for relaxation or contemplation, for 'getting away from it all', catering for needs quite the opposite of the old country farmer's, who, having worked in the fields all day, found his recreation in turning his back on nature to contemplate the intimate scale of his hearth.

Baggy House

The three Hudson houses considered here are all about view, and all occupy privileged country sites. Baggy House has the best position, the kind most architects can only dream of. Dramatically placed on the north Devon coast looking both towards Baggy Point and back across Croyde Bay with a huge sky and surf rolling in from the Atlantic. It owes its right to exist to a nineteenth century predecessor built by the proprietor of the *Birmingham Post* and subsequently converted into a small hotel.[2] Hudson and his clients thought at first of retaining the old building, but decided the conventional structure with flat floors and a single front was unworthy of the site, so all that has been preserved is a couple of retaining walls. To exploit the widest angle of view the new house was planned instead as a projecting corner facing two views at right angles: south across the bay and west towards the point. The equivalence of the two faces was celebrated in a square-centred plan with the living room as focus, set at first floor to be halfway in section as well as in plan. This square, and a larger concentric one embracing the outdoor terrace, are clearest in the first floor plan, with dotted lines to indicate the curved canopy roof which unifies the corner. The turned timber column, sole support for the floor above, celebrates

Baggy House.

the diagonal, which passes on through the corner 'sea room' with a panorama of nearly 180 degrees, a kind of prow or forecastle. The glass sidewall both there and in the adjacent dining room drops entirely into the floor, turning inside to sheltered outside, but one steps up a level from dining to living room, looking out and over in both directions, with more light admitted from the generous clerestorey. At the heart of the house one can turn around to enjoy the hearth, which has an appropriately focal position, its chimney providing the house's key vertical accent from without.

To gain the best angle of view, the whole house turns in plan 23 degrees from the old retaining walls and contour line, which gives the north-projecting wing a skewed edge and sets the garage on the skew, differentiating the angle of approach and movement from the stasis of the primary square. Crucially, the divergent angle reappears in the entrance hall, causing it to expand towards the choice of route, then absorbing the turn of the main stair as it rises to meet the living room head-on. Hudson admits that concern with the experience of movement was a priority, and has written of being captivated by Adolf Loos and the concept of the *Raumplan*.[3] He avoids axial progressions in favour of progress around the side, which he recognises as a special quality of Islamic architecture.[4] At Baggy House the route clings to the north and east edges of the focal square, first rising to a landing over the entrance hall. This looks out on a small northern courtyard, an intimate sheltered spot in the bosom of the hill to contrast with the threatening vastness of the other side. After the glimpse of courtyard, the route turns again to rise southwards on glass treads past guest rooms to a projecting balcony at second floor, a crow's nest with the most exposed view of all, a vast openness. The ground floor offers alternative routes: one from entrance hall westwards via study and playroom to garden, the other indirectly sideways into the kitchen, facing its breakfast corner and views of Croyde Bay, with more steps to be discovered up to dining and down to playroom. All views available to the house are framed and offered in contrasting ways within an unfolding visual narrative that knits the interior into the setting, and this also gave the *raison d'être* for the exterior.

From the approach side the house is relatively solid and defensive, dominated by the tapered chimney which is at once flue, ventilation and lightwell. The white solid-looking forms, though in fact hybrid and abstract, look load-bearing and,

Baggy House.

Light House.

with their sometimes very small windows, evoke a seaside vernacular. Seen from the west the building is quite different, much more open, and commanding a long flat garden terraced into the hillside.

The north end continues the vernacular vocabulary with white wall, slate roof, tiny windows, and even a projecting bay reminiscent of the Arts and Crafts; but the south end is all glass, with turned up copper canopy in celebration of the corner. It is a roof rampant rather than couchant, its gesture of openness contained by flanking turret-like solids that enclose the edges of the canopy roof and celebrate that primary square in the plan. A third such solid turret masters the south elevation, again articulating an internal line of passage: this time the westward route from kitchen to dining room and on the same line as that to the guest room above.

Comparison with other houses

If one good test for contextual architecture is to consider whether its site needs it, another is to see whether it could equally be placed elsewhere. Hudson's Baggy, Light, and Bavent houses are so very different that the idea of them swapping sites is preposterous just in terms of style and massing, let alone issues of topography and view.

Light House in Belper is also on a hillside commanding a good view of the town and hills beyond, but the situation is steeper and more linear, and it looks due west rather than south. To make the best of the view the big living room is in the upper floor looking out also on a garden to the south, while principal bedroom and bathroom take the north end. The east, buried in the hill, is a sunken court and car port, partly roofed. Fearing the stringencies of old age, the client demanded a flat floor for all main accommodation, turning the whole house and its arrival court into a plateau, in contrast with a six metre level change across the site. The demand that the view be preserved for the houses behind prompted the need for a low roof, and if it had been horizontal to accompany the relentlessly orthogonal plan, the house would just have been a box. But the flat roof slopes with the topography in both directions, rising towards the south and west, closing to north and east. It is clad in stone slates to be seen: Hudson calls it the "fifth elevation". Its dynamic form also rhymes with the modified topography of the drive which sweeps through in a loop, the car being accepted

Light House.

Bavent House.

as the universal means of arrival and dramatised as with the Villa Savoye—in contrast with Baggy's coastal path which the car invades on sufferance.[5] Like Baggy, Light House offers contrasting encounters with its view in different places, hiding it away at first by the enclosure of the sunken court, then suddenly revealing it on entry. The fully glazed dining corner, in many ways the climax, looks both south and west with garden steps from the south end, but it has big sliding doors to view and west, one of which hangs beyond the corner, opening the room wide onto the wooden balcony. The bedroom has a balcony too, and dividing them, in the middle of the west side, is a projecting glazed bay. This allows a 180 degree angle of view and collects sun on winter days, and at its rear at high level small windows open from a tiny study, another version of the crow's nest or eyrie.

Bavent House is different again, built on a relatively flat site that was part of an old farm. In its levels it is a conventional two-storey house with living rooms on the ground and bedrooms above. The difficulty of the site was that the best view—of wilderness and estuary—lies to north and west, while the approach and other buildings lie to the south, along with the sun. Unlike the earlier examples, this house has little sense of immediate enclosure and needed to generate some of its own, so it has an articulated form departing from the right angle to make a series of local 'places'. The long straight side facing northwest follows the site boundary and enjoys the view, while the south has projecting corners, leaving a kind of waist between for a dining room which can face both ways and becomes the centre of the whole.

It expands southeastward into a small court sheltered by the north wing, which also cuts off the living space from the realm of cars. The kitchen and utility area at the ground floor are raised by a step in a form of spatial punctuation which makes visitors step down into the main social rooms, and also gives increased height to dining and living rooms beyond. The staircase rising in the north wing reaches the south across a bridge which is also a study, with a crow's nest view of the estuary through a well-placed window opposite. All this is local, specific, and with a different scale relationship to its site than the other houses. The three are also materially distinct, for Bavent House echoes the barn it replaced with much timber siding, and stands intentionally rather barn-like in its landscape, but Light House is set into its hill, so is materially all about stone retaining walls

Bavent House.

Salvation Army.

which echo the old quarry on which it was built. Baggy House, in white render, on the other hand, was clearly an added object in the landscape, from one side echoing the vernacular, from another the heroic period of Modernist abstraction.

Rural and urban

It is often assumed that the country and the city are opposites and strangers, with different rules for their architecture, yet the city is also a topography, has views and progressions of space, fronts and backs, and the questions of neighbourliness are often more pressing. To contrast with the three houses I add an urban building with a more social purpose to show how Hudson's approach copes equally with this and with a much more modest budget: the Salvation Army church and social centre on the edge of Chelmsford. The site is caught between the Medieval road running southeastward out of town to its north and the modern dual carriageway to the south, and remains of the original Roman road were actually found beneath. The Salvation Army's previous building from the 1960s had occupied the site object-like, surrounded by left-over space used largely for car parking, and was in poor condition. Hudson chose to replace it by filling the site to make best use of the land, placing the church in the east and creating a courtyard for outdoor activities on the west, a space not originally requested by the clients, but which has proved enormously successful. Regretting the damage to the town done by the ring-road, the council is seeking to restore the memory of the historic main road at least as a pedestrian link, so Hudson placed his main entrance and canopy on the north side, with a welcoming glazed foyer inviting everyone in. By contrast the south side is closed and clad in metal but with an added turret of coloured glass marking the altar which reveals a cross to passing motorists, and is simply designed to be perceived at a glance. The end east wall of the church, set in a small linking street and open to passing pedestrians, has been inscribed with biblical quotations on a red background which one can linger to read. Built of laminated timber panels on a tight budget, the church was a much cheaper building than the three houses considered earlier, but it reflects many of the same principles, including careful deployments of interior space and use of varied types of window to pinpoint particular local views.

Conclusion

The habit of seeing buildings as objects extracted from context is perpetuated by presenting and judging them in the daily press in the form of a single photographed

Baggy House.

Salvation Army.

1. Ulrich, Roger S, "View Through a Window May Influence Recovery from Surgery", *Science*, 1984, pp. 224, 420–421.

2. Information from written description by Anthony Hudson, 2012, unpublished.

3. See Risselada, Max, ed. *Raumplan Versus Plan Libre*, Delft University Press, 1988.

4. Risselada, *Raumplan*, 1988.

5. Le Corbusier's Villa Savoye at Poissy near Paris of 1929 is the key example: see Blundell Jones, Peter, *Modern Architecture Through Case Studies*, London: Architectural Press, 2002, pp. 111–122.

6. It originated with Alexander Tzonis and Liane Lefaivre but was famously taken up by Kenneth Frampton in his seminal *Modern Architecture: A Critical History*, London: Thames & Hudson, 1984.

image. This accompanies a tendency born 60 years ago with mass-production that pushed architects to repeat the same building on different sites and even in different countries. A parallel form of mass-production developed with large scale modern practice which soon discovered the ease and economy of copying and adapting existing designs to completely new contexts, sometimes even without the bother of visiting the site, which was probably distant anyway. If you don't visit the site you can't know about the views, the light, the neighbours, the history, memories, or anything else local, and your building is likely to end up autistic. This is why it is necessary to differentiate buildings, so that each responds in some way to given conditions and they are all different. It is harder work and more expensive, perhaps the reason why three of the examples here are luxury houses for which the design time can be paid, but the fourth case showed no such privilege in pursuing the same ends. We have been talking about critical regionalism for 30 years now in reaction against the notion of an international style, but making buildings belong to place requires much more than adopting a few stylistic features borrowed from the local vernacular: it means somehow re-establishing or even reinventing local roots.[6]

Opposite Perched above the dramatic Devon cliffs, and with south-facing and angular form, Baggy House perfectly reflects its rocky and coastal environment.

Right The living and dining rooms give stunning framed views of the bay and open sea beyond. Photograph taken with full-height glazed walls in their down position.

BAGGY HOUSE

LOCATION: North Devon, UK.
DESCRIPTION: New build six bedroom family house.
DATE: 1994.

The country retreat has always focused predominantly on the sensate experience of living; the enjoyment of sun, the play of light on surfaces, the framing of magnificent views contemplated by day and night, social engagement and relaxation. This is the central theme of Baggy House inspired by Pliny's description of his Laurentine Villa on the Tyrrhenian coast. He gave a powerful image of what the house could be. "You may wonder", he says, "why my Laurentine place is such a joy to me, but once you realise the attractions of the house itself, the amenities of the situation, and its extensive sea front, you will have your answer...."

The house nestles into rising ground to the north (right) whilst opening up to spectacular views of the Atlantic to the south and west.

Pliny continues with words that unerringly describe Baggy House sitting on the north Devon coastline. It has "... a small but pleasant courtyard; this makes a splendid retreat in bad weather... and then a dining room which is really rather fine; it runs out towards the shore, and whenever the sea is driven inland by the southwest wind it is lightly washed by the spray of the spent breakers. It has folding doors or windows... so that at the front and sides it seems to look onto three seas, and at the back has a view through the inner hall, the courtyard... to the mountains in the distance... a little further back from the sea is a large bedroom, and then a smaller one which lets in the morning sunshine with one window and holds the last rays of the evening sun with the other; from this window too is a view of the sea beneath, this time at a safe distance... (another) bedroom enjoys the bright light of the sun reflected from the sea... there are living rooms, as well as (the) dining room which command the whole expanse of sea and stretch of shore."

The west elevation copper canopy over-sails the living areas and fully glazed walls. The solid white rendered elements of the house contain the bedrooms, giving privacy and security.

The site is exceptional: elevated on cliffs with a panoramic view of the Atlantic. Baggy Point, a promontory on the north coast of Devon, was chosen in the nineteenth century as a site for a house by the founder of the *Birmingham Post*. The building later became a hotel and the present owners bought it to restore it to a house. Although a significant landmark it had little architectural merit and as the living spaces had no view of the sea it was decided early on in the project to build anew. The brief was straightforward: to create an informal

family house that made the most of the spectacular location. They had no fixed ideas of how the building might be; in fact they were courageously open to all possibilities.

The site's characteristics are contrasting: closed views to the north where the ground rises steeply, with open views to the east, south and west. The house responds to this with two faces. The northerly, opaque and contained under slate roofs, takes shelter from the rising ground. The southerly,

Opposite From the southeast the two faces of the house can be seen. The house opens out southwards (left) with large areas of glazing whilst to the north (right) forms are closed. The distinctive chimney makes reference to both local vernacular architecture and ships.

Left The oversized chimneys of local vernacular houses mark the front door, an element of traditional design that has been incorporated into Baggy House.

Right The copper-clad canopy over the dining room mediates between the views and living room and extends out over the terrace. The pre-patinated internal and external finish suggests an external living space, which exists when the glass wall is lowered into the ground below, emphasising the connection with the surrounding landscape.

transparent with angular forms, projects towards sea, cliffs and jagged rocks below. These contrasts are in tandem with environmental and structural strategies: the north with thick tapered masonry walls of high thermal mass and small windows, the south with the light-weight timber, steel and glass benefitting from sun, light and natural ventilation. Walls are over-clad in white rendered insulation referring to the whitewashed vernacular of Devon.

The appearance of the house externally is not a direct correlation of the interior. To some extent the reading of the interior is intentionally obscured to hide its secrets and give privacy and, as with classical buildings, the exterior elevations have their own compositional story to tell. For example the south elevation intentionally keeps the window sills and heads to a constant height

despite changes in internal floor and ceiling levels. The northerly elevations shield the more private rooms (bedrooms, bathrooms, study and gym) from an adjacent house, formerly stables, overlooking them. This is the solid face that greets you on arrival concealing the sea views and giving privacy to the interior. These are compact forms, taking cues from the local building vernacular with thick battered walls, slate roofs and small windows giving discreet views of the land and seascape. A massive chimneystack, which marks the front door, can be read as a familiar local vernacular arrangement or ship's funnel. The front door leads through to a low hall with lead-clad ceiling, an English grey sky, and a rough hewn granite column alluding to the granite rock strata below but supporting the chimney above. Bright shafts of light flood down the staircase drawing one towards the airy living spaces above.

Top left In summer southwest-facing glazed walls can be lowered completely into the ground dissolving the boundary between inside and out. Glazed walls up.

Bottom left Glazed walls down.

Right The fireplace and oak paneling in the living room form an intimate, relaxed and luxurious corner of the house. Surrounded by the other rooms, the living room forms the central space of the house. The guest glass staircase has viewing holes, seen here high on the walls. To the right a balcony overlooks the kitchen.

These are located on the southern side with views across the sea. A patinated copper-clad timber canopy surrounds the central living room acting as a loggia over the dining area and external terraces and emphasising continuity of space from inside to out and views. This literally occurs when, at the turn of a key, the full width glazed screens descend into the ground revealing the living room as an open pavilion looking out across the Atlantic Ocean. A single column sited in the centre of the main space is the sole structural element that supports two sides of the living room. In its inverted tapered form and laminated construction, the smooth surface and lightness, it is a total contrast to the granite dolman in the entrance hall. The living room is the link between the two elements—the opaque and the transparent, the solid and light. It is the centre and heart (with hearth) of the house around which

other rooms radiate in plan and section: the dining room to the south, kitchen to the east, playroom below (the kitchen forming a kind of halfway house to them all), guest rooms above and family bedrooms to the north. The complex relationship of rooms, one to another and each with their own character, responds to the needs of home life and opens up many narratives for family and guests to play out their time there. This idea, inspired by Adolf Loos' notion of the *Raumplan* and so wonderfully employed in the Müller House in Prague, is central to the enjoyment and use of the house. Other than the main entrance into the living room there are no major axial routes through the house. Circulation is consistently on the edge of rooms giving prominence to inhabitation of space over passage through; something that Islamic architecture was a source for as was the surface treatment.

Top Like a ship mast, a single timber column supports the living room ceiling on the south and west sides. Each structure in this space is visually separate from one another; column, copper canopy and aluminium light shelf all enhance an open-air feeling and draw light into the house.

Bottom In the entrance hall under a lead-clad ceiling, a granite column supports the chimney above. Pyramidical in shape, this column is the antithesis of the sitting room timber column, reinforcing the juxtaposition and graduation of contrasting elements, textures and themes that characterise the house; lightweight and solid, open and closed, above and below, warmth and coolness, modern and ancient.

Left A vaulted ceiling and oculus reflect the semi-buried position of the main bathroom to the rear of the house.

Right The main bathroom, in semi-buried position and enveloped by vaulted ceilings with oculus and turquoise tiles evokes a Turkish bathhouse; silk curtains screen off the bedroom.

The boundaries of a room are defined by emphasising the finishes: glazed ceramic tiles, rough render, smooth plaster, patinated lead and copper, the grain of natural materials, polished or rough, all play a crucial part in the choreography of the building. Climbing up through the house, from the 'cave' of the entrance hall to the eyrie-like top floor, the house becomes lighter in feel. This spatial journey is emphasised by a progression of surfaces from rough to smooth: floor finishes go from riven slate to polished, from stone to wood and finally from wood to glass, used to form the stair treads to the top floor guest bedrooms overlooking the shimmering stainless-steel roof and sea. From here an external bird-walk runs seawards exposing intrepid viewers to the full fury of the elements. In contrast the family bedrooms are set back from the sea, shielded within the solid part of the house

as it merges with the rising land. Vaulted ceilings cocoon the rooms with the main bathroom resembling a Turkish bath-house.

The building plays with a choreography of materials that heightens the experience of each room and its place in the house. Equally it plays with metaphors and makes much of the realities of the local vernacular, landscape and orientation simultaneously binding them into an architecture that celebrates day-to-day living and therefore of its time and place.

BAGGY POOL

LOCATION: North Devon, UK.
DESCRIPTION: New outdoor pool garden to Baggy House.
DATE: 1997.

Hidden from view within the grounds of Baggy House is a small sunken garden. Here sits the pool: the only clue to its existence is a pink wall peeking over the stone enclosure to the main garden.

Previous page Isolated and private, the perimeter of the pool is surrounded by stone walls and a tamarisk hedge. Rising ground to the north gives views over the pool and out across the bay to the southern coastline.

Top left Cantilevered white concrete steps connect the pool to the upper garden.

Bottom left Elliptical pre-cast concrete seats, dining table and worktop sit on a plinth overlooking the pool, perfectly positioned for barbequing and entertaining.

Top right Water from a cascade falls into the pool providing movement and a good place for a dousing.

Bottom right View back towards the house. The pink screen wall separates the pool from the main garden. To the right oversized stones create a visual breathing space against the boundary wall.

A slate causeway divides the pool in half and sits just below the water line with a tunnel beneath connecting the two sides of the pool. Timber deck, stone pebbles and tamarisk hedge on the boundary behind.

This pink wall forms one end of the pool enclosing changing rooms with a terrace above. It is also a canvas: incorporating steps dropping down to the pool deck where a platform and diving board hover over the water beside a cascade.

The pool is split into two parts by a black slate causeway; sitting just below the water level it heats up in the sun and people paddling across appear as if they are walking on water. The larger area is for general swimming and diving with the smaller and shallower children's pool containing seats. Though distinct, the two parts of the pool are connected by an underwater tunnel below the causeway allowing intrepid swimmers to pass from one side to the other.

In contrast to the house, where materials become more refined as one progresses skyward, here materials and surfaces become more polished the closer one gets to the water; from concrete paving on the terrace to polished limestone within the pool. Around the pool terrace, growing out of the natural contours of the site, two curved walls enclose a dining platform with a barbeque and a spiral-shaped shower enclosure which looks like a nautilus shell. In the shade of the stone boundary walls with their crown of tamarisk large rounded stones adorn a narrow strip alongside the pool: an Alice in Wonderland pebble beach.

Opposite In the sunken entrance courtyard, a circular opening above brings light and respite, and a cool shallow pool offers a sense of harmony and reflection between the interior and exterior worlds.

Below A clear progression of materials can be seen from right to left; there's a physical story-telling of heaviness and lightness, from the solid red quarry stone anchored to the hillside through to the lightweight steel balcony overlooking the valley.

LIGHT HOUSE

LOCATION: Belper, Derbyshire, UK.
DESCRIPTION: New build four bedroom family house.
DATE: 2005.

Light House sits on the site of a former stone quarry, high on the valley side looking west and south across the Victorian mill town of Belper and to the distant hills beyond the River Derwent. It is visually tied to the remnants of the quarry with stone, and reaches outwards towards views and the landscape with a lighter-weight structure. This is a horizontal equivalent of moving through a house vertically, from basement to attic, whereby one knows one's position in the house by the way it looks and feels.

Top left The distinctive tortoiseshell patchwork slate roof mimics the agricultural pattern of the fields beyond.

Bottom left First sight of the house is from above, seen against the valley and town of Belper in the distance.

Right The northwest slate-clad elevation protects the house from the Derwent Valley winds, while remaining visually elemental.

Having lived in the area for many years while building a thriving business, and now with a family grown-up, the owner, Jackie Lee wanted a house that could literally work on two levels. The upper entrance floor is her domain: living, kitchen, dining areas, bedroom, bathroom and utility room all function like one large apartment. Despite the steepness of the site, this part has no level changes as Jackie wanted the option of living in the house into old age. Downstairs are three bedrooms for visiting family and guests.

The house is approached from above so the roof is a highly visible part of the building. With a covenant restricting its height to preserve views from houses already built behind, the roof has a very shallow slope in two directions: south down to north with views to the valley, and from east to west dropping with the land. It becomes the fifth

elevation to the house with a chequerboard of slate tiles forming a visual link to the patchwork of fields seen across the valley. The roof then folds down the northwestern elevation, further encapsulating the house and protecting it from the prevailing winds. The whole effect looks elemental with the large slates riveted to and concealing an inexpensive industrial corrugated roof.

Stone screen walls form a retaining wall to the hillside and enclose the entrance forecourt. Heavily rusticated, they are a memory of the quarry face that once stood there but also form a protective and secure space. The slate-clad roof over-sails forming a *porte-cochère* and so connects house and garage. In order to create a moment of respite by the front door there is a circular cutout in the roof that frames the sky and brings light down to the lower level.

Top The open plan kitchen sits behind the main living space commanding views beyond and to the south.

Bottom The view beneath the carport towards the front door; the forecourt here is protected and enclosed by rusticated stone walls which commemorate the former quarry site.

The dining and living rooms open out together on to the balcony, giving dramatic views of the valley below. Further down the two-storey 'floating' sunroom extends out to the south over the sloping ground.

The main entrance leads past cloakrooms and kitchen to the living areas and finally, on the south, to a balcony stretching the full width of the house that makes the most of views and orientation. Reflecting the progression from solid quarry face to lightweight balcony, from north to south, the construction and finishes progressively get lighter and more refined; moving from load-bearing masonry to steel frame, from stone finishes in the hall and kitchen to timber and stainless steel in the living area around the fireplace; from small north-facing windows to large expanses of glass overlooking the valley. The roof overhang cuts out high summer sun but also visually extends the interior space southwards onto the balcony. Large glazed sliding doors open up towards the views with the east corner hung from a cantilevered arm similar to aircraft hangers.

The most significant element in the progression from heavy to light, north to south is a cantilevered double-height sunroom projecting five metres out from the house giving dramatic views up and down the valley. It sits between the living room and main bedroom and, as the only part of the house that breaks the horizontal roofline, so becomes a significant element in articulating the house's form and the origin of its name. Partly inspired by a Julius Schulman photograph of Pierre Koenig's Los Angeles Case Study house with the city lights stretching out beneath one's feet, it also contains memories of the owner's childhood holidays in Cornwall sitting in sunrooms and balconies. Concealed behind the sunroom a stair runs down to the lower floor and to the upper mezzanine cabin office: an eyrie that has commanding views in all directions. This arrangement also provides natural stack-effect ventilation using floor vents in the sunroom and the high level windows in the eyrie.

Through the staircase lobby is the main bedroom that connects to bath, shower

Right The stone-clad bathroom evokes a Pompeian atria, but is also a translation and adaptation of the client's nostalgic memories of a bathroom she fell in love with in the Far East.

Left An oak staircase connects the lower ground floor bedrooms to the main living areas and rises up to the eyrie above the sunroom.

and steam room. Top-lit, it is reminiscent of Pompeian atria but also a bathroom that Jackie fell in love with in the Far East, though now adapted to the English climate. Clad in the same stone as the rest of the house, though more refined by being honed, it suggests security and privacy similarly afforded by the other stone elements of the house.

The house is a narrative that not only deals with moving from solid to light, from quarry to suspended sun room, but also one that weaves memories of the owner's past with the needs of the present and the future.

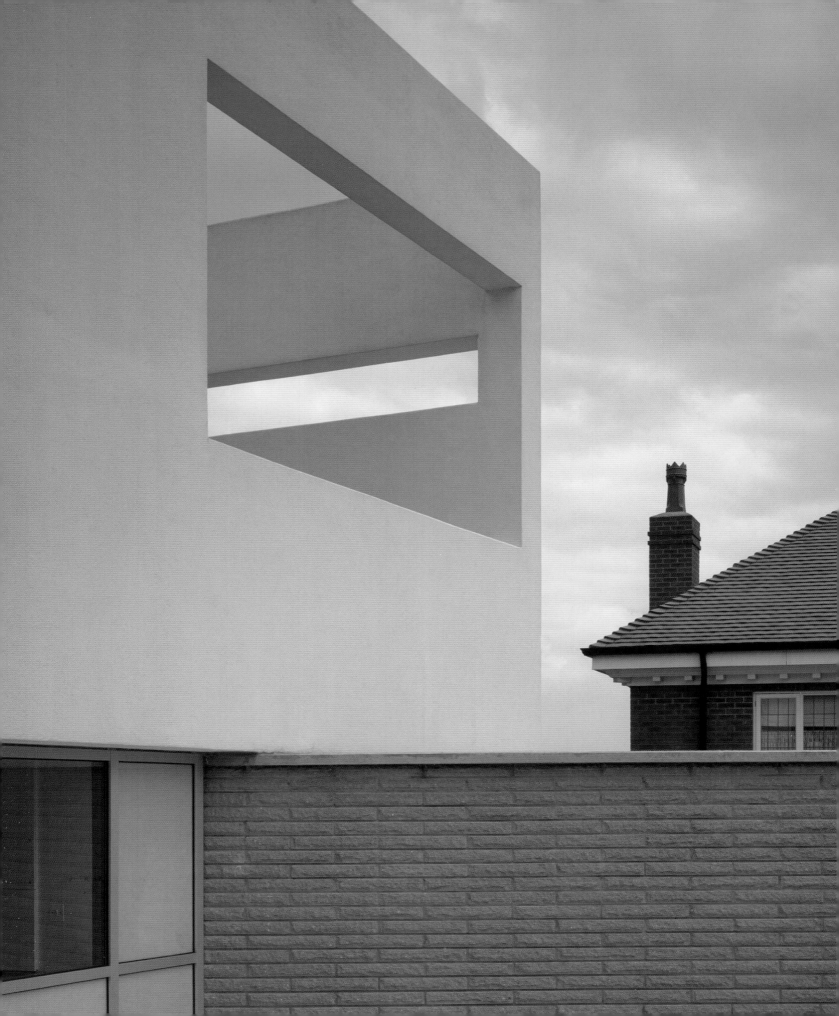

DROP HOUSE

LOCATION: Northaw,
Potters Bar, London, UK.
DESCRIPTION: New build four/
five bedroom family house.
DATE: 2000.

The suburban house has held a fascination for the English, if not for many architects. This was an opportunity to look at how a late twentieth century suburban house might be treated and how the suburban ideals of light, air and nature might be replayed. The plot was one of five that were being developed simultaneously, sitting just inside the M25, near Potters Bar, and surrounded by houses following a typical suburban pastiche. The owners were determined to avoid this and wanted something that made the most of the site and modern technology, had a contemporary character and, most importantly, provided them with a comfortable family house. Northaw Park, the estate within which the development is situated, has at its centre an Italianate white stuccoed nineteenth century villa which sets another cue: the Modernist villa with the precedents of Le Corbusier's Villa Savoye, which became a leitmotif for the project.

Previous page left Two suburban contrasts: Drop House is a contemporary exploration of the suburban house type.

Previous page right Approached from the south and set back in the plot within Northaw Park, the house is a visual oasis of calm composure.

Top Seen from the wood to the rear and north of the house the building fragments into a loose composition of forms. From left to right, the curve of the garage, projecting television room sitting above the ground floor guest room and living room.

Bottom Below the cantilevered first floor the front door is marked by a section of the 'drop'. Enmeshed in the house it forms a constant reference point throughout and contains all the water elements of the building.

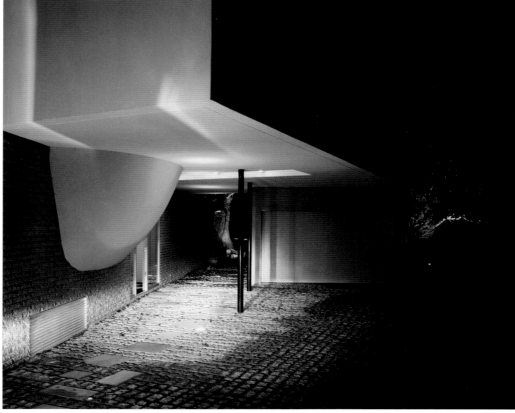

Tucked in front of the woodland, here the south front of the house apparently floats above the fully-glazed garden level. The living spaces are open and light in contrast to the floor above where space is predominantly closed and private.

The plot is south-facing with a wood to the north. All other developments took a conventional approach by placing the house towards the front with grand car-turning circles leaving, sunless and dead, north-facing gardens to the rear growing moss. Instead, Drop House sits at the rear of the plot closely embracing the wood without endangering trees thus leaving generous room for a south-facing garden. The land slopes gently upwards from east to west and this is exploited in the various levels of the building. Arrival is at the lowest point of the site under the cantilevered first floor, also partly supported at the rear by the garage

whose curved rear wall marks out the turning circle of a car. Entering into a small hall from under the house one encounters an elliptical shape that gives Drop House its name: an egg form that rises through the house that reappears on every level. It contains all the water elements: baths, showers, sinks, lavatories and washing machine from which 'grey water' is harvested and stored in a tank under the garage. From the hall a stair rises through the house wrapping around a top-lit, tilted wall which alternates between feeling open and closed depending on what side one is on. The lower part is broad and processional, washed in light leading to the

Left Painted plywood panels in the living room suggest a cross-section of the building, while various openings give views of the stairwell, dining room and, at high level, a workspace.

Right On reaching the first floor landing, daylight floods one side of the stair wall while the other moves into shadow towards the bedrooms. The juxtaposition of light and dark, solid and lightweight, open and enclosed all play out carefully throughout the building.

family rooms, whilst the upper is cocooning and intimate leading to the bedrooms.

Playing with the various levels gives each room its own appropriate proportions but also maintains a visual relationship with each that corresponds with the various territorial demands of the different family members and activities—whether a high ceiling for the living room, a double-height galleried library or a low cosy ceiling for television watching. Many views and circulation routes further break down a standard suburban formality so that the family, wherever they are, feel part of the whole and share in the life of the house.

The main living area opens directly onto the south terrace and garden with a sitting alcove at the farthest extremity. Northwards it looks into the canopy of oaks. From the living room a ramp leads to a small purple

quilted den for television and computer games that can be opened up or closed off from the house via sliding doors. The adjacent library has a similar arrangement as well as having its own dedicated door off the main staircase. The bedrooms are more conventionally enclosed, but to get to them there is still a sense of moving round enclosed or open spaces that makes the house fun to explore. On the cantilevered corner of the house the main bedroom looks out onto a south- and east-facing terrace into which the drop cuts; here it opens into the bedroom where it is experienced to its best effect as a big curved soft space housing the bathroom. The walls are punctured with circular glass lights that recreate the effect of a Turkish hammam with penetrating rays of sunlight. Squeezed between the drop and two straight-forward children's bedrooms is their bathroom with a resulting curved

Top Both the living (on the left) and dining areas open out onto south-facing sloped terraces making the most of the gentle slope of the site.

Bottom At the rear of the living room and facing the northern wood a ramp leads up to a snug quilted space designed for watching television. To the right a sliding door hides or opens to a library.

Top The 'drop', partly projecting into the south bedroom terrace, contains the master bathroom, where glass lenses cut into the walls transmit shafts of light into the interior.

Bottom A collage of different materials is incorporated at the rear of the house to emphasise a sense of informality; cement panels fitted glass, aluminium and render all give the cross-section, an exposed feel.

Texture plays an important part in giving a particular character to each room. Here knapped concrete blocks form the flank wall of the living room.

corridor. Beyond these, at the end of the journey through the house, is a small workspace that looks down into the main living room and out towards the approach road, keeping an eye out for any visitors.

In the spirit of suburbia, inexpensive materials have been exploited in special ways giving texture and a narrative to the house both internally and externally; the rusticated concrete brick walls ground the house on west and east sides forming a protective bastion off which the lighter timber frame is constructed. This is clad in acrylic-rendered external insulation relating to the original stucco villa in the park. The internal wall of the living room is clad in painted plywood panels in a pattern that

hints at the function of the room behind; horizontal stripes for the library and an arrangement that suggests beds and desks. It is as though the house has been cut through and its interior has been exposed.

Throughout the building the design has changed the normative design of the typical suburban house into something more modern and relevant. The 'drop' replaces the Elizabethan turret of the house next door as the external 'must have' feature whilst the interiors undo the stultifying conventions that have become the hallmark of suburbia.

PUSHPANJALI

LOCATION: Delhi, India.
DESCRIPTION: New build three bedroom family house.
DATE: 2005.

This project in Delhi for an extended Indian family and staff was not only concerned with their immediate needs but also with the legacy of Hindu building practices, the influences of Islamic architecture and their western interpretation.

The area of Puspanjali in southwest Delhi was previously farmland. As the city expanded, farms were parcelled up into large individual house plots. A wealthy Delhi construction family owned one on which they wanted to build two family houses; one for each of two brothers with guest house and staff quarters.

Mughal miniatures, often portraying landscapes and buildings, provided one inspiration for the project. The setting took the nearby Aravelli Hills to the south of the city as it subject with the high stone boundary walls forming the picture frame. This rolling landscape has been reinterpreted in three dimensions as a series

of linear mounds that form a backdrop to the whole site—a contrast with the flat land surrounding it. Under these mounds are concealed service areas, stores, garages and staff quarters with their own private courtyard.

The Hindu owners wished to adhere to some of the principles of Vaastu, a cultural code for building, similar to Feng Shui but much more specific regarding what can or cannot be done. It is a Hindu 'art of building' that contains many truths but has been so codified that many of its 'rules' have lost their practical significance. Nevertheless there is much that is familiar and sensible in the way buildings

Previous pages Inspired by the palatial Mughal buildings of Northern India, the north front of the house appears as a fortified wall, with small window openings. The curved entrance canopy leads to the front door and beyond a glazed turret gives access to the roof.

Top The living room rises to almost three storeys with clerestory lighting on the north (right) and curves down to the south, extending to views out over the garden.

should be rooted in their context through landscaping, the placing of rooms, how you should approach a building, where you should enter (from the north), what parts should be heavy in construction (again the north) and what parts should be lightweight. The building is also influenced by Islamic architecture using the practices and practical know-how of dealing with the hot climate by keeping the internal environment of the building pleasant despite extreme summer temperatures.

Although two houses, a tented guesthouse (reflecting the transitory nature of visitors), and a health club were planned, only one house was realised according to the original design. This has the ideal orientation, with its entrance on the north elevation, a south-facing garden and the landscaped 'hills' to the southwest; an important location in terms of Vaastu. The entrance leads to the

main reception space under a vast billowing convex roof that not only accommodates living space but also houses the owners' collection of Indian artefacts and modern paintings. The roof is double-skinned, insulating the interior from the summer heat by air flowing between the two leaves. Many Mughal buildings of Northern India use this simple concept to keep internal temperatures bearable. Off the main space are smaller, more intimate rooms and alcoves again inspired by Mughal domestic architecture. Bedrooms and more private areas of the house are arranged around an internal courtyard that brings in natural light.

A significant difference between building in the West and the East is the differential cost between labour and materials. Whereas in the West labour costs are proportionally higher than materials, in India it is the reverse. This

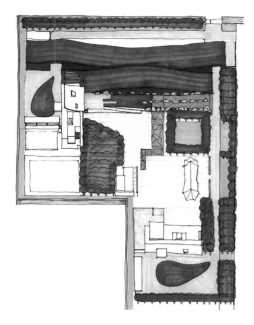

Left Sketch of the site showing (to left and bottom) the original layout in the form of a Mughal painting. The two houses, (central) health club and guest tent, (top) and rolling landscape concealing store rooms.

Top right South-facing, the living room roof shades the terrace and cascades towards the garden, protecting interior and exterior spaces from the intense summer heat.

Bottom In the centre of the house a tall courtyard attracts light. The bedrooms all lead off from this central space, giving a sense of openness leading to privacy and calm.

means that considerable value can be added by working and manipulating materials; stonework can be done in an intricate manner (it is difficult, however to get good quality workmanship) and time can be spent getting things right. The north-facing walls are of dressed and shaped stone with horizontal slate bands similar to local building tradition and other modern interpretations, such as Joseph Stein's exemplary Delhi International Centre. These walls form a protective enclosure to the north and east. To the south the building form breaks down into separate elements that address the garden: a corner pavilion,

the large roof overhang and terraces that shade family living areas and bedrooms. These areas are for living and have richer textures and surfaces that respond to the interior of the house. This was furnished by Abu Jani and Sandeep Khosla and reflects the Indian love of colour and richness of materials.

It is a family house that celebrates Indian culture in its contents, the way the building sits in the context of the plot, and its layout and construction.

BAVENT HOUSE

LOCATION: Reydon, Suffolk, UK.
DESCRIPTION: New build
four bedroom family house.
DATE: 2010.

Exposed to the full blast of North Sea winds, Bavent House turns an awkwardly orientated site into a positive attribute making the most of magnificent views across reed marshes, open countryside with glimpses of the sea. The internal layout and character of the rooms respond to this and at the same time these give the owners, Richard and Lucy Turvill and their daughter, Clix, a home that enriches family life and effortlessly accommodates frequent guests and extended family. Originally part of a small farmstead that had been split into three, the site had been occupied by a modern barn and sits alongside the farmhouse and redeveloped farm cottages.

Previous page left On arriving in the entrance hall, the interior is revealed in a series of angled planes, giving differing perspective views through the house.

Previous page right The south elevation is 'cracked open' like an egg, opening it up to sun and revealing views. A soft inner lining of timber paneling contrasts with the harder zinc outer shell.

Below The north entrance is conventional in form with black zinc cladding, forming a protective shell from severe weather. The house elevation kinks to make the most of the northerly views.

Sites in open countryside that have a difficult orientation inevitably place greater demands on the design and arrangement of spaces than those with more ideal aspects; but of all orientations the most awkward is having amazing views to the north contrasted with dreary ones and arrival to the south. Bavent House has all three.

People and cars are directed to the house's front entrance past the retained farm buildings, now used as stables for Lucy's horses, and skirt around the south of the house. Facing north, this formal elevation resembles a child's drawing of a house

and is also inspired by fishermen's huts on Southwold's shingle beach nearby. It also exhibits a slight kink and change of direction where the orientation of the house itself twists to make the most of the views. The black zinc cladding is a carapace protecting the house from buffeting weather and refers back to the black-tarred finish of fishing huts. Carved out of this skin are timber-clad pockets of space that catch the sun and provide views alongside shelter from the weather. Of these, the largest is the south-facing courtyard which creates a U-shaped building form to give views through the house towards the marsh. The other spaces around the edge similarly

Top Inspiration for the external shape and materials were found in the black-tarred fisherman's huts on Southwold beach.

Bottom On the west elevation the zinc roof over-sails providing protection from winds and a sheltered spot to sit on sunny evenings. The timber-clad areas of the house contrast with the zinc carapace.

Overleaf The northwest elevation is skewed towards the marsh and gives the roof a distinctive silhouette. Each face of the house has its own narrative.

Opposite top The arrangement of the windows demonstrates how light is captured and brought into the house. A clerestory above the double-height dining space brings in morning to afternoon sunlight, while the first floor windows on the mezzanine watch for arriving visitors.

Opposite bottom The northwest elevation makes the most of the views. Windows (left to right) top: master bedroom, mezzanine beyond, guest rooms. Bottom: kitchen, dining room and living room.

Left The stairs from the hall leads up to the double-height first floor landing and is lit by a rooflight that traces the sun's path, mimicking a sundial.

Right The view from the kitchen with mezzanine above, the dining room below and beyond through to the large living room. Each individually distinct room, communicates with its neighbour, giving the house a network of open and connecting areas in which the family can exist alongside or separately from one another.

provide havens depending on wind, time of day or season. These potentially inhabited spaces have a softer treatment with the use of iroko timber panelling that has faded, mimicking the colour of surrounding reed beds. Thus the overall simple form of the house, distorted by the shift in orientation and the external 'cut-outs', gives it a distinctive silhouette; playful and picturesque from some viewpoints, formal from others.

The interior uses the different orientation and angle of wall planes to give shifting views and routes through the house giving a dynamic relationship between the rooms and spaces. The focal point at the centre is a double-height dining room, emphasised by the first floor balcony and study space overlooking it. This is sandwiched on either side by two wings of the house that wrap around the courtyard. The westerly wing has a large living room

with guest bedrooms above, while its easterly counterpart contains the kitchen, snug, utility spaces and entrance hall sitting below the family bedrooms. The main staircase off the hall was fabricated off-site from steel and appears as a bridge to the first floor, set against a translucent polycarbonate wall that brings natural light into the guest cloakroom and first floor bathroom. At night this is reversed when back-lit.

This compact arrangement allows the family to remain in touch with each other as they go about their daily lives. There are also places for privacy, such as the snug that projects out of the house or the alcove in the main living room, a favourite place for Lucy's father. Bedrooms sit under the pitched roofs, whose gentle slope in two directions provides a rich variety of spaces beneath: the lofty master bedroom, Clix's large room with a mezzanine

Opposite The steel fabricated stairs refer to maritime ship construction, forming part of the ongoing visual language of the house.

Top left The master bedroom, in the north corner of the house looks out on to stunning views of the marshland beyond.

Bottom left A bath with a view: the bathroom vista extends across the marsh towards the North Sea horizon.

Right First floor landing looking towards the master bedroom and mezzanine.

to accommodate friends, or the cosy guest bedroom in the western corner of the house where the overhanging eaves reinforce a sense of shelter and protection.

Internal finishes are simple to emphasise the geometry of the different wall planes; mainly of white painted plaster and highlighted at significant places with muted timber panelling. Oak handrails with slate and bleached Douglas Fir flooring further emphasise the house's sculptural qualities. This harks back to an overall feel that Lucy Turvill expressed a love for: Richard Ede's house at Kettles Yard, Cambridge where the sculptural qualities of the space are enhanced by the use of simple materials. Responding to a wonderful but difficult site, Bavent House, like other houses before it,

continues to explore the relationship between the exegesis of needing an understandable, readable exterior with an interior that is rich with spaces and rooms of varying volumes, character and relationships. While working with a reduced palette of materials it embraces the complexities of family life and provides a stage onto which this can be positively played.

MAKING

THE VERNACULAR ARCHITECT
SARAH WIGGLESWORTH

QUAKER AND HALL BARNS

FEERING BURY BARN

ALPES-MARITIMES

56 STOREY'S WAY

CHANTRY FARM

CEDAR HOUSE

A straw bale wall in Hall Barn; fiberglass panels are bolted on to a lightweight metal frame creating a subtle veil over the straw they protect.

THE VERNACULAR ARCHITECT

SARAH WIGGLESWORTH

Quaker and Hall Barns.

Feering Bury Barn.

Open Youth Venue.

Paul Oliver defines vernacular architecture as being culturally and anthropologically specific in time and place and characterised by an "economy in form and design, clarity and simplicity and the unabashed, undecorated use of materials".[1] Conventionally we have associated this definition with the folk buildings of traditional cultures and craft-based techniques. But as globalisation and industrialisation have undermined these traditions, recently writers have come to recognise the vernacular in the informal, low-brow and everyday architecture produced under professional structures and capitalist building systems.[2] These buildings are the unselfconscious works that make up the "background type".[3] I would like to argue that one important strand of Hudson's work could be described as a "modern vernacular".

By using this definition I am not referring to the borrowing of naive imagery, the imitation of received archetypes or the romantic reference to features, details or design strategies that derive from historical precedents, nor even to a nostalgia for past processes and production, although all of the above have made minor appearances in Hudson's work. The vernacular, in this context, refers to ways of doing that could be called opportunistic, which is to say that they exploit affordances offered by the site (including cultural and spatial references) while employing technologies that are easily available and ready-at-hand, that are economical and that are of their 'place'. In the context of a capitalist product-oriented building materials market, such a technical vocabulary can encompass the sort of kit you can buy at the local B&Q; or the bits of gadgetry floating around the house, the yard, the neighbourhood or the farm; or the product which has reached the end of its original purpose and can be put to a new use. By extension, therefore, the category includes the reuse of entire buildings.

It is perhaps in the buildings that are reused that this approach can most clearly be seen: Quaker and Hall Barns projects, where existing redundant stock is remodelled to new purposes relevant to the twenty-first century (in this case, holiday homes) or at Feering Bury Barn, which became a home and artists' studios. At the Open Youth Venue in Norwich, which is a more urbane remodelling of a listed former bank, Hudson selectively alters the existing building and adds new constructions that create something new and relevant to its young occupants. Across every project can be found small, clever innovations: the inventive employment or reuse of elements intended for other purposes. A window handle is borrowed from a Morris Minor (Quaker and Hall Barns); straw bales from a local farm are used

56 Storey's Way.

Cedar House.

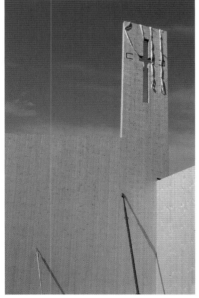

Salvation Army.

to provide a cheap walling in Quaker and Hall Barns; polycarbonate sheeting underlies traditional glass roofing tiles (Quaker and Hall Barns, Feering Bury Barn); and the signature flat glass that relies for its waterproofing solely on the use of neoprene and silicone pointing (56 Storey's Way, Quaker and Hall Barns, Cedar House). This technical daring is a refreshing antidote to a world of architecture increasingly restricted by performance standards and certification schemes. Hudson is interested in working with the given but he is also interested in testing and experimenting with ways of building and, in the process, reinventing traditional processes in line with modern technology. However, whereas conventionally, such techniques would have evolved over long periods of time, being improved and adapted with each generation, in the span of a single career this experimentation must, by definition, remain in the realm of the prototype, sometimes working, and sometimes, annoyingly for the user, not.

In parallel, there are projects (Cedar House, Salvation Army) where the construction uses off-site fabrication and 'just in time' delivery systems, employing factory-fabricated 'modern methods of construction' as the technology. While this type of construction is vastly different from our idea of a local or regional architecture, it could be argued that it represents a vernacular because it uses ready-at-hand, standard products available through catalogues, selected and arranged to the designer's edict. Redeemed through the precision of factory fabrication, skills and making are possibly less critical here than the juxtaposition of signs and signifiers.

Importantly, the way of working encompassed by this approach does not discriminate, as we did in the twentieth century, between species of technologies. In Hudson's work, the timber could originate from a state-of-the-art factory in Austria; the window could be the best Danish engineering but ironmongery could be recycled from an old door; or the worktop for a kitchen could be the flagstone that was found under a barn. The common thread linking these ideas is Hudson's desire to explore the creative possibilities across building types, eras and ways of making, firmly situated. This is a method that permits a fluid, playful and contingent interplay between the architect, the client and users.

In this endeavour, the Feering Bury Barn comes as close as possible to the ideal of the craftsman/designer in the mould of William Morris. Here, Hudson's design strategy made use of components from the former barn building while externally

Feering Bury Barn.

Cedar House.

the (new) roofing solution recalled the appearance of commonplace agricultural buildings, used partly to satisfy Heritage Officers. The client/owner of the barn undertook to manage the contract, procuring the subcontracts, prototyping and later carrying out much of the work himself. An artist with skills ranging from drawing to wood- and metal-work, and possessing a clear aesthetic of economy, he saw virtue in the well-used, the familiar and the valued, extending this aesthetic to using offcuts from the roof to clad the walls, and employing the much-loved but scored plywood cutting board to make panels in the master bedroom. In this work, the make-good-and-mend economy has been taken to new heights and craftsmanship elevated to the status of art. The results are knowing but not scholarly, deep but not overtly serious; yet they are simultaneously clever, canny and crafty.

At Cedar House, which employed SIPS panels as the technology, the building structure could be erected in a matter of a week or so, and it allowed large openings in unusual places. The form of the building references minor farm buildings, which can be found in the vicinity. These are cleverly presented to the visitor on arrival just before reaching the house. But the differences are also marked: Cedar House is raised up on sleeper walls so it hovers above the flood plain, and it is not built of brickwork. The shingles are an oddity in the context of local traditions that glean their materials from the ground (brick, clay tiles, flint). This is not so much a house of the earth but an ark that could float away. Perhaps this is a new vernacular: one that recognises the future under global warming.

It is tempting to see something of Hudson's background in his work. The son of a pig farming family from North Walsham, Hudson is immensely practical and has the farmer's knack of putting all things to good use. Widely travelled and brimming with curiosity for places and artefacts, Hudson is able to draw on a vast reserve of references across place and geography. In combination with an irreverance for convention, he employs his sourcebook of references in witty and playful ways. Originating from Norfolk, living in Norfolk, and dealing with Norfolk architecture therefore, Hudson represents a new type of regional architect, one that brings thoughtful, original approaches to the East Anglian context, raises regional quality and asks powerful questions about place, identity and matter.

One definition of a vernacular is that it does not involve architects. Rather, it is made by those people that are expressly not professionals, drawing on archetypes to meet needs and desires within clearly defined cultural boundaries. In pre-capitalist eras the connection between deep-rooted cultural values, symbolic systems and place were not subject, as they are now, to forces of globalism and branding. Architects, by definition, are conscious manipulators of symbolic capital, knowingly participating in a conversation transcending place and time (geometry, abstraction, ideality). At its root, to be a professional demands the kind of objectivity that takes one out of place and out of time. Yet at the same time, architects are conscious of their professional complicity with forces that remove us from place and time, that deliver technically-driven solutions that are the same throughout the world; that are bland and culturally unspecific while doing huge damage to the environment. Hudson is part of a generation seeking new answers to the dilemmas brought about by modernism.

Accepting that once work enters the compass of professionalised architecture it might no longer be classified strictly as 'folk' building, the compelling question raised by Hudson's work is whether it is possible or even desirable to speak of a "modern vernacular" in the context of UK architecture. Hudson's work, and the sorts of work his practice attracts, comes perhaps as close as any architect can to the definition of a modern vernacular.

1. Oliver, P, *Dwellings: the vernacular house worldwide*, London: Phaidon, 2003, p. 11.

2. Brown, R and Maudlin, D, "Concepts of Vernacular Architecture", in CG Crysler, S Cairns, and H Heynen, *The Sage Handbook of Architectural Theory*, pp. 340-368.

3. Till, J, and Wigglesworth, S, "The Background Type", in *Accommodating Change*, ed Hilary French, London: Architecture Foundation/Circle 33, 2002, pp. 150-158.

QUAKER AND HALL BARNS

LOCATION: Haveringland,
Norfolk, UK.
DESCRIPTION: Barn
conversion to two houses.
DATE: 2001.

A small number of architects have undertaken their own developments and become their own client. This gives a unique opportunity to try out ideas, experiment and challenge some of the orthodoxies of designing and building, as well as observe how the buildings perform with less fear of the repercussions if things don't quite work out. Converting Quaker and Hall Barns into holiday accommodation was a chance to do this.

Previous page left A new staircase leads to an overhead walkway spanning the existing oak framed bays of Hall Barn. To the left the lime rendered straw bale wall provides a highly insulated and breathable wall that help maintains an ideal internal environment.

Previous page right Hall Barn (foreground) and Quaker Barn (background) enclose an entrance forecourt.

Left The south elevation of Hall Barn with the new bay. This projects from the existing building encapsulating large areas of glass in direct contrast to the solidity of the original barn.

Right Straw bales fit within the bays of the original cart shed. On the roof bespoke rooflights re-use the original glass pantiles in conjunction with an inner double-glazed unit.

The buildings, which form an 'L'-shaped footprint, were part of a larger complex of disused nineteenth century farm barns. They were converted into two homes and are currently rented as self-catering holiday accommodation. To allow freedom in decision-making the construction process was project managed rather than having a main contractor. The principle followed was to use local labour and skills and, wherever appropriate, local materials. Minimal drawings were produced initially other than floor plans so that the design could adapt to changing circumstances and details could be drawn up as and when they were required. This flexibility meant it was easy to deal with unknown defects or problems, fine tune details according to local skills, make the most of materials available and, out of necessity, 'cut the coat according to the cloth'.

The two barns are distinctive: Hall Barn was a two-storey, oak framed, open bay cart shed with grain storage loft while Quakers Barn was a single-storey cart shed of little intrinsic interest. The most significant adaptation of Hall Barn was filling in the north-facing open bays and opening up the south-facing blank brick wall to views and a newly created garden. Infilling the five bays with straw bales was

the obvious solution since wheat was growing in nearby fields. Once sprayed with borax to treat against insect infestation they were easily installed in panels, held upright between the oak posts and pinned together with steel rods. Bale-shaped openings framed by plywood boxes were created to allow light into the building. Each bay was then over-clad with a lightweight steel-supporting framework made locally, with translucent fibreglass sheeting bolted over. This stops rain but also throws a subtle light through the straw bale openings with shadows from the steel frame adding to the veil. To ensure a long life to the straw, copious ventilation was allowed at the base and top using high duty stainless steel mesh to prevent vermin from making their own home within. Internally the walls are lime plastered which allows them to breathe: all in all one of the cheapest walls you could wish to make.

The only element that breaks the form of the original barn is a single-storey bay structure on the south side. This contains large glazed openings facing the garden with sliding doors which, when fully opened up, disappear into a slot that forms the back to a cosy inglenook sitting area within the double-height living space.

Top View from the living area in Hall Barn towards the dining area and kitchen with the new walkway above. The barn retains the open plan feel of the original building.

Bottom The bespoke windows were all sourced and made locally: a small steel framed casement window to the bathroom, a sliding steel window using gear from Landrover windows, and sliding oak doors to the living room.

Overleaf The barns' gardens all face south overlooking an open expanse of countryside. Hall Barn (to the right) and Quaker Barn (to the left) remain true to their original nineteenth century forms.

Left Hall barn living area. The curved first floor landing in the shape of a pulpit encourages a sense of theatre.

Right View from 'pulpit' over the living area in Hall Barn.

The overall effect is to keep the 'barn' qualities of the building that are so often lost in conversion: one of simple forms and minimal openings. The roofs have no rooflights in the conventional sense but use glazed pantiles, a common feature of Norfolk barns. By adding a secondary glazed unit there is little heat loss and protection from the weather. Further experiments were made with the windows that are loosely based on Landrover window lights, a Landrover Mark II being the inspiration as well as a workhorse on the project. Frameless double-glazed units slide in simple steel tracks, draught-proofed with Landrover window seals all screwed to

the brick walls. This was another simple semi-agricultural detail developed to avoid the look that robs barns of their uniqueness as well as having the advantage of being cheap to make locally by a metal fabricator.

Internally the two barns are treated differently. Hall Barn exploits the simple oak construction and puts this on show whilst Quaker Barn, which had less points of interest, focuses more on new surface finishes such as tongue and groove panelling and a knapped flint wall. Marble chips laid in resin are a floor surface suggesting chalk, another distinctive material found in Norfolk and, helped by underfloor

Quaker Barn: A newly constructed top-lit knapped flint wall forms a backdrop to the dining area.

heating, provides a deliciously warm and textured surface to walk over barefoot. In Hall Barn, a first floor 'bridge' runs across the middle two bays, through the double-height living space and connects the main bedroom to the stairs. It forms a gallery with, at one end, a curved pulpit forming the stairs landing adding playfulness to the interior.

Because the existing buildings had moved considerably over their life, nothing was square or plumb so the design had to take account of big tolerances and misalignments, something that modern detailing often cannot cope with. Each element was therefore designed as 'loose-fit', as and when needed, but always determined by the available materials, tools and skills on the site. In this sense the construction process has created two contemporary vernacular buildings.

FEERING BURY BARN

LOCATION: Feering, Essex, UK.
DESCRIPTION: Grade II listed barn conversion into two bedroom family house and workshops.
DATE: 2011.

The relationship between design and making is fundamental. Woven into this equation is ensuring we value our resources—both material and human. It is therefore important in a world of diminishing resources that we place more emphasis on thoughtful application and invention that in turn puts a high value on the way we work. This is the central focus for the conversion of Feering Bury Barn into a home and workplace. How do you make the most of a lovely but dilapidated sixteenth century timber-framed barn with all the accretions that have occurred in its lifetime and how do you value the workmanship that goes into it?

Previous pages left The southeast gable wall. In order to remain faithful to the original structure, the windows occur only within the historic openings of the barn.

Previous page right The sixteenth century aisled oak frame of the barn is lit by the new rooflights, which are invisible from the outside. Within the structure recycled concrete silos are used to separate the main living space from the bedrooms.

Right Internally the rooflights are obvious and bathe the interior with light. They consist of a weathering layer of transparent, corrugated roofing with multi-walled polycarbonate panels below providing the insulation, all supported by the barn rafters.

Opposite top The agricultural appearance of the barn is uncompromised. Expanded galvanised metal mesh covers the barn roof completely concealing all the roof lights below whilst letting in an abundance of natural light.

Opposite bottom Southwest elevation: the strong roof form of the barn is kept intact with no visible openings. A predominant factor of the design was to maintain the integrity of the former structure.

Overleaf Northeast elevation. The accretions and remnants of 500 years of farming have been left intact, but modified to suit the new life of the buildings as home, studio and workshops.

It is an unusual project because the owners developed the detail design as they worked on the building themselves. Of all the work in this book Feering Bury Barn is the most collaborative venture between architect and the builder/designer owner. Ben Coode-Adams, one of the owners, brought not only his skills as carpenter and metalworker to the project but also an enormous sensibility to the design process. He attached huge value to using materials in a responsible way—in particular the value created by the action of the human hand and mind.

Ben and Freddie with their daughter, Willa, planned to move to Essex from London. Both needed workspaces to replace those left behind and, because space was also needed to house a vast collection of toys and found objects, the project became a living display case alongside a house and working studios —in a sense a small Pitt Rivers Museum.

The barn was part of Ben's parents' farm and had lost its original purpose as a store for grain and equipment. Nonetheless, the remnants of that history littered the building inside and out: externally corrugated sheet silos, redundant out-buildings, Dutch barn and, inside, 1950s precast concrete silos and numerous bits of old machinery. Wherever possible all this was to be recycled, given a new life and celebrated. Whereas others might have stripped away the modern accretions and sanitised the buildings, Ben and Freddie wanted to keep the unbroken history.

As with any barn the secret is to maintain the simplicity of form so as not to undermine its integrity. Being Grade II listed and a spectacular oak framed structure (if not a little rotten), the local conservation officer was even more adamant that no rooflights should be visible in the roof and that no new openings, other than those already made, should appear in the walls. This had thwarted all previous attempts to get listed building permission for a house conversion so a roof covering was devised that appears to have no rooflights yet floods the vast interior with natural light. The secret was to use an expanded metal mesh that sits above large rooflights. This acts as louvers, allowing light into the building from above while obscuring

Left Two of the eight concrete grain silos within the barn were dismantled and re-erected. They now enclose bathrooms and a spiral staircase. The floor is a polished concrete slab.

Right The kitchen sits at the end of the main living space against a full-height glazed screen, which separates it from the studio beyond.

all views of glazing from ground level. The mesh came in galvanised square sheets and were 'T-washed' to give them a darker tone. The overall effect was remarkably similar to the previous bitumised corrugated roofing on the barn but has a beautiful patchwork quilt look which changes hue with humidity. After agreeing the principle of the roof construction, Ben developed the detailing so that it could take up the irregularities of the timber structure and this is apparent in the gracious undulations of the new roof.

Use was made of every existing opening in the external walls to get light in and views out; these included the original barn openings but also breaches made by previous farmers to take the latest bit of machinery, be it a flue or extract for corn drying. The walls were stripped back to the timber structure and then reclad using planking cut from storm-damaged

willows from the farm as an internal lining. This was then built up with insulation and over-clad in feather edged boarding.

Reuse of everything, from the large to the small scale, was an essential part of the project. Two of the internal concrete silos were re-erected to screen bedrooms from the main space with enclosed bathrooms and a spiral staircase. This permits privacy and private space, while still allowing the main barn to be seen as a whole. The external corrugated steel silos will be adapted for guest accommodation. Moving down in scale, parts of the Dutch barn were reused to strengthen a full-height glazed screen wall that separates living space from studio space. At the minute scale all hardwood off-cuts from timber repairs were used as a sculptural fire stopping between floors. Ben's view is that anything that has been worked

Left Stairs to the main bedroom. Solid oak steps supported on a purpose made metal chassis spiral up and within the concrete silo.

Top right Parts of abandoned agricultural machinery and equipment have been re-used; here to fabricate ties and brackets in order to stiffen the weaker parts of the deteriorated barn structure.

Bottom right Timber off-cuts were re-used and wedged together to plug gaps between ceiling joists.

Above The main bedroom is screened from the rest of the barn at first floor by the silos. The gap between forms a balcony overlooking the living space below. Note that the cutting board for tiling has been used as a balustrade at the top of the spiral stairs.

Opposite Nothing was left unused; here cupboards were made from packing cases recycled from the move out of London.

on has added value from that process and that should therefore be both recognised and celebrated. A favourite example is a plywood cutting board for tiles, now the spiral staircase balustrade, which is an abstract pattern of blade incisions.

The overall approach to restoration was a mixture of straightforward conservation and repair to the timber structure mixed with homespun interventions using disused bits of machinery and metal work. It is a time-honoured idiosyncratic tradition and the way a farmer might repair a barn in their often 'ad hoc' way. Decisions about how something

was to be built were governed by the skills of the people available on the project, the restrictions and availability of the tools to do the work and the cost of materials. This narrowed down some opportunities but, at the same time, by applying intelligence, economy and imagination, it has led organically to a highly-crafted and special building. This has many lessons for the building industry in using our resources, both material and human in a responsible way.

ALPES-MARITIMES

LOCATION: France.
DESCRIPTION: Conversion of existing farmhouse and villa into a single nine bedroom family house.
DATE: 2009.

Two separate and contrasting buildings, each with their individual characteristics, have been brought together as one large family house for entertaining. Working in France added further rich layers to the design process since French building trades are organised differently to British ones: employed directly by the client this allows the architect to benefit from the trade's individual craft expertise without the filter of a main contractor. In turn a direct and positive relationship means details can be honed and developed throughout the building process.

Previous page left The *mas*: the view through to the older part of the house captures the organic spirit of the original construction; uneven battered walls and rough textures reinforce this character.

Previous page right Two parts of the house sit side by side. To the left the nineteenth century *maison de maître*, to the right the eighteenth century *mas* connected by a new dining room. In the foreground an outdoor living area and pool overlook the mountains and sea beyond.

Left In contrast to the more rustic *mas*, the dramatic bathroom in the classical and formal *maison de maître* is an echo of the French Baroque.

Right The dining room with polished plaster ceiling forms the central visual link between the two parts of the house.

Opposite In the *mas*, tectonic qualities of modern concrete construction were exploited; the roof was cast from the waney-edged timber boards that now clad the end wall, forming cupboards and paneling.

Located in the foothills of the Alpes-Maritimes above Cannes in the south of France this involved a major refurbishment of buildings which, by accident of history, were two distinct houses: a eighteenth century farmhouse, the *mas*, alongside a nineteenth century villa, the *maison de maître*. The two-storey *mas* is one room deep and of the local vernacular with no wall straight, while the *maison de maître* is modelled on a typical classical house: two rooms deep, foursquare and with high-corniced ceilings. In bringing the two buildings together to create a comfortable family home, the architectural priority was to emphasise each building's separate character as well as making the house into a whole.

The buildings are locally listed which meant there could be little change to the exterior elevations; however there were no restrictions to internal works and rearranging the accommodation. Family bedrooms are located on the upper floors of the *maison de maître* with smaller guest bedrooms in the *mas*. Living spaces are also split between the two in a way that complements each building's character: formal living areas in the *maison de maître* and more informal spaces in the *mas*. Since the buildings were gutted and roofs were completely rebuilt it was possible to exploit new construction to refresh their identities. The new concrete roof to the *mas*, in particular over the kitchen area, makes particular use of French concrete expertise. Concrete is cast on waney-edge timber shuttering and, when struck, it reveals a beautiful and highly textured surface resembling an upturned boat. Reclaimed timber from the shuttering was cleaned and re-used for wall panelling; a subtle reminder of how the roof was constructed as well as emphasising the rusticity of the *mas*.

In homage to the character of the original *mas* the battered walls are retained and the plasterwork and joinery of the original building inspired the new detailing: plasterwork is the background and frames

Top left A lap pool sits alongside the unheated plunge pool.

Bottom left The gap between the two buildings once formed the main entrance to the house, leading to the church on the far side of a now busy road. This gap was blocked up to make the link between the houses and now opens up to the garden and outside living area.

Right Pergolas provide shade and frame the pool. A succession of outside living areas, complete with cooking and dining facilities, are positioned for admiring the wonderful views of the Alpes-Maritimes.

The entrance to the house was re-orientated to the western terrace above a car parking area. The new doorway uses stone dressings salvaged from a locally demolished building.

all new joinery. It is used sculpturally to form soft and curvaceous recesses and shelves. All corners are hand formed without plaster beads giving the sense of the spaces being scooped out of the body of the building; something that French plasterers, though resistant at first due to their Cartesian culture, were very adept at.

In contrast the timber-roofed *maison de maître* is treated classically with rectilinear room cornices and opulent detailing. The rooms are more sumptuous, using polished stone. Doors are panelled (mostly reusing the original ones) rather than boarded. Similarly, the plasterwork is sharp and walls flat rather than irregular. The main bathroom shows the contrast with the *mas* to best effect with polished marble and a hint of French Baroque flamboyance.

The final piece of the jigsaw ties the two different buildings together making a whole of the parts: this is the gap between the two that originally provided access to the church across the main road through a stone arched opening. The gap is now breached by the dining room, forming the fulcrum to both the house and garden. The ceiling in polished plaster runs through into both buildings and draws them together. From the outside the join is treated as a recessive element so to keep the respective identities of the two buildings, while the roof provides an external link between the first floors of both buildings. In summer the glazed doors can be opened fully to the garden.

The garden is as a series of different outside rooms. Fronting the *mas* is a pool and outside living area with space for sitting, cooking and dining on a lower terrace. Pergolas provide shade with extendable canvas awnings that frame landscape views of olive trees, mountains and sea. From the car entrance on the lower terraces of the garden steps lead up to an external garden lobby and thence to the new front door. Constructed of reclaimed stone quoins from a nineteenth century doorway, it has a Bacchus-faced keystone.

Through the skills of French trades the character of the two original buildings has been enhanced, while the new house offers appropriate formal and informal spaces for family and guests to enjoy the pleasures of sitting on the edge of the Alpes-Maritimes.

56 STOREY'S WAY

LOCATION: Cambridge, UK.
DESCRIPTION: Single-storey extension to existing Grade II listed house.
DATE: 2010.

Adapting and extending existing houses to suit the needs of modern lifestyles is necessary to revitalise our building stock; however it becomes more difficult and sensitive when working on a house that has a strong architectural pedigree by a significant architect. 56 Storey's Way by the well-known Arts and Crafts architect Baillie Scott presented such a challenge.

Previous page left The new pavilion provides a foil to the Baillie Scott house which can be seen through and behind it.

Previous page right The minimal structure and frameless glass walls are capped by a projecting canopy, which provides surrounding shade. The simple shape visually refers to the bold roof form of the house.

Above A glazed walkway floats above the ground and connects the pavilion to the house.

56 Storey's Way is one of his more modest houses but interesting nevertheless. Much has changed socially since it was designed in 1923; for instance the convention then was for reception rooms—the domain of the family—to be clearly separated from staff quarters such as kitchen and utility areas that were the domain of servants. In the intervening years, servants and this separation have disappeared and, in the case of 56 Storey's Way, these rooms at the east end have been taken into the rest of the house and used as the family kitchen and dining room. Thus inevitably the focus of life has ended up at the service end consequently changing the

overall balance and occupation of the home. The brief from the current owners, Professors William Marslen-Wilson and Lolly Tyler, was to address this and to add a day living room while at the same time removing a former heavyweight extension applied to the original garden loggia. The owners were particularly keen for the remodelling to make more of the garden and sun as the existing reception rooms are low-ceilinged and relatively dark.

The new room is treated as a glass pavilion sitting to the rear of the existing house. It dovetails into the original loggia, which in previous alterations had been opened up

Positioned in the south-facing garden, the new extension has an asymmetrical relationship with the house, complementing the original internal layout.

through to the kitchen and dining area beyond. The pavilion is all but separated from the Baillie Scott house other than by a glazed connection that docks into the loggia recess. The roof, walls and floor to the connection are glass and bridge over the outside paving as the ground floor is slightly raised. As a bridge from house to pavilion this lends a little drama as one moves from one to the other across the gap. This little detail also restores the original threshold between inside and out.

The pavilion structure is designed like a 'table top' supported by freestanding internal legs,

allowing fully glazed walls so that the house can be seen through and beyond. A generous projecting canopy whose shape reflects the inverse silhouette of the main roof shades the glazing, which is frameless to achieve maximum transparency. A brick plinth of similar tones to those of the house emphasises the perimeter of the pavilion while oak double doors frame the original loggia behind.

The overall design is a quiet, unfussy addition that sets off the original building, adds some drama while also making sense of the changes that have occurred in modern day lifestyles.

Opposite Facing northwards over a shallow river valley, Chantry Farm sits adjacent to Denton Church and Rectory.

Right A walkway inserted into the original structure shows the marriage of new and old. At a high level, mirrors fixed to the internal partition dramatically reflect the internal structure, visually replicating the original length of the barn.

CHANTRY FARM

LOCATION: Denton, Suffolk, UK.
DESCRIPTION: Grade II listed barn conversion into five bedroom family house.
DATE: 2011.

It is a well-established architectural concept that introducing contemporary designs into old structures generates a visually and texturally rich building: the juxtaposition between the old and new. However, for this to work successfully it is important to have a clear understanding of what gives the existing structure its character— what is the dialogue between the old and new trying to communicate?

The original large barn openings now relate to the main living spaces: in the centre, the kitchen and to the right, living room, both of which open onto a southwest facing terrace.

Chantry Farm is a Grade II listed timber framed barn in Suffolk that had been left redundant and was beginning to fall into disrepair. The owners of the building, Alan and Laura Jarvis and their daughter, Holly, wanted a conversion that kept the character but was also contemporary.

Part of a bucolic setting of farmhouse, church and barn, it presented quite an imposing black timber-clad structure set at the point where the land slopes away to the fields beyond. The original seventeenth century barn had been extended over the course of time to become two large barns set perpendicular and at different levels to one another, and the low brick plinth walls had been repaired roughly, typical of a working agricultural building. Internally the original timber frame was generally sound and its lack of external openings created a real sense of enclosure and protection from the cold easterly winds.

The key characteristic was its rough functional nature with large simple internal volumes. The trick was to somehow create the human-scaled spaces for a family home while retaining the sense of it as a barn.

Externally, the idea was to change the existing appearance of the barn as little as possible: the only significant modification being the removal of a recent single-storey lean-to extension to the barn and creation of a new single-storey extension added to create a new entrance. Other than that, insulation was added and timber boarding was replaced, the roof re-tiled and the plinth walls left as undisturbed as possible. Existing openings are retained and the number of new windows minimised to avoid the 'domestication' of the building so that the building still reads as a barn rather than a house. Rooflights are concealed behind reclaimed glass pantiles and some new windows are concealed behind glass slats that continue the lines of the external timber boarding.

Left Off the kitchen a dining area looks north over the entrance area.

Right An overhead walkway crosses from the stair landing to the main bedroom allowing the main volume of the barn to be seen as a whole. It also acts as a canopy over the kitchen work surfaces.

Entering the barn, however, reveals a completely different and very contemporary character. Two large full-height volumes, one to each barn, display the full extent of the historic timber frame with all its irregularities, markings and worn texture exposed against the clean light and smooth surfaces of the new plasterboarded walls and ceilings. In the first of these, the Upper Barn containing the kitchen and family dining area, there is a long elegant bridge leading to the master bedroom hovering above the kitchen island units. High level mirrors reflect the roof structure to re-create a wonderful sense of the original volume. An angled wall with highly glossed panels leads you down into the Lower Barn to the second full-height volume with the sitting room, before continuing to the new free-standing fireplace wall with its dark grey polished plaster that feels strangely like velvet to the touch. Both of these two volumes have the original projecting bays with new large glazed screens to each elevation set within the existing openings

(one side high, one side low) typical of Suffolk threshing barns. The walkway and the fireplace not only provide clear orientation to the open plan layout but also respond to the scale of the volume and continue the narrative between the existing and new. To heighten the drama of these volumes the timber framing to the walls and the plinth is hidden in the single-storey areas, a strategy that also prevents these becoming too visually 'busy'.

Two winding oak staircases lead from the entrance hall up to the bedrooms: one for the family and the other for guests. The walls of these rooms are also lined but the roof structure is left clear to soar above the spaces—utilising the drama of the structure but on a more intimate scale. Clear lines of sight right through the building help to strengthen the sense of the single volume, and carefully positioned windows extend these further to give a light and airy feel with a good connection to the world outside.

Top View from the living room up to the entrance hall. To the left are further steps to the kitchen and dining area.

Bottom Oak staircase from the hall to family bedrooms.

Opposite Within the original volume of the barn the historic timber frame has been kept. Inserted within this are modern elements; a screen wall and fireplace separates the living room from the snug beyond.

The construction details were developed to be fully breathable in order to preserve the longevity of the existing timber structure, and to emphasise the design strategy of creating a narrative between old and new. For instance, the straight and plumb frames of the modern aluminium windows are deliberately set clear of the uneven and raw existing framing. Similarly the straight back edge of the sill board to the plinth is kept clear of the existing wall-plate highlighting its irregular edge and simplifying the construction process: it would have been a difficult job to trim the boards to follow the existing timber and the distinction between old and new would have been weakened. The finish of the timber frame is left rough and untouched to contrast against the even textures of the lime plaster, the smooth highly glossed panels and plinth sills, and the monolithic appearance of the limestone flooring.

At Chantry Farm a historically significant building has been sympathetically converted into a contemporary home. The 'old versus new' concept works particularly well here because of three key decisions: to contrast the inside from the outside appearance, to not just retain but to exploit the large volume within the building, and to emphasise the texture of the historic timber frame with careful detailing and specification of materials.

CEDAR HOUSE

LOCATION: North Elmham, Norfolk, UK.
DESCRIPTION: New build two bedroom private house and studio.
DATE: 2004.

In the past, prefabrication and low budget housing have been given a bad name in the British construction industry for being unadaptable and impersonal. More often than not if someone has a plot and is looking to build a prefabricated house they will tend to look at the various continental kit systems on offer which give limited potential for adaptation to a particular site or client's brief. Cedar House shows that prefabrication does not have to be so restrictive; in fact it can open up a surprising number of possibilities and innovations that can be exploited to suit the particularities of a site.

Previous page left The house has been reduced to the essential elements of construction, expending with gutters and such like. The projecting galvanised metal window cheeks throw water off the glass whilst cedar shingles provide an overall cloak.

Previous page right The studio and garage are at the north end of the house. Being on a flood plain the high level window is required as an escape hatch in case of flood.

The photographer client of Cedar House, Paul Gyseman, bought a chicken shed on the River Wensum flood plain with planning permission for conversion to a house and work space. However, both the location and condition of the shed were far from ideal; the shed, some distance from the river, was collapsing and liable to flooding. So a new permission was obtained closer to the river and raised off the ground to reduce the flood risk. The most significant challenge, however, was to build a house and photographer's

studio with a low budget and fine tune the house to its location.

It was clear right from the start that both a simple volume and construction system would give the best chance for these objectives to be met. A single-storey building on a rectangular footprint with pitched roof was adopted, containing separate living and working areas at either end sandwiching a bedroom and bathroom section. The form is very familiar in the Norfolk landscape

View of southeast corner. Arrival is from the left and the River Wensum is to the right with raised vegetable beds in the foreground. The cedar shingles have weathered in this photograph.

where barns abound. Architecturally it was important that the roof space should be part of the interior, so various construction systems were investigated with the structural engineer—resulting in the choice of a panelised prefabrication system. Through clever engineering it gave the building an unobstructed roof space with no ridge beams or purlins since the structure acts as one large diaphragm tied together with a timber ring beam at eaves level.

The location posed its own challenges with the best views of the river to the northeast, an approach from the south and the need to elevate the building one metre above likely future flood levels. The optimum orientation for the house gave a west-facing terrace and entrance platform with the best framed river view on the northeast corner. It asked for a corner window and the engineer discovered that this could be done with the adopted construction system as well as an eight metre opening in the west wall overlooking

Opposite The living room opens up onto a west-facing raised deck, which also acts as the entrance platform for the house. This area runs towards the river as a pontoon, making it an ideal place to sit out in the evening.

Top The best views are from the northern corner of the house. Here the opportunities provided by timber frame construction are exploited to the full allowing a frameless corner window.

Bottom The gable end panel of the house provides enough stiffness to form a cantilever allowing the open corner.

Opposite View of the northern corner from the river reflected in the River Wensum.

Top left The small budget required making the most of the building system. Behind plasterboard linings, the raw panelised roof construction is visible and creates distinctive areas within the house.

Bottom left The studio at the north end of the house includes a mezzanine above the garage. It also provides access to the window that can be used as an exit in times of flood.

Right The kitchen to the left, entrance to the right with wood-burner in the centre of the living space. Note the sacrificial wall linings to the left.

the terrace. This allows the living spaces to have fantastic views and to spill out onto the terrace when the sliding-folding doors are fully opened.

To further reduce costs external details and finishes were simplified. Because the building is raised off the ground all gutters and rain water pipes could be removed. Only one external finish of cedar shingles was used, giving the building a unity and boldness of form similar to barns with the occasional punched opening. Shingles are one of the cheapest and most ecologically sustainable materials because there is very little waste.

Internally the majority of surfaces are finished in plasterboard although the lowest one metre of the walls is lined with sacrificial timber panelling which can be easily stripped out in the event of an unusually high flood that is predicted to occur in one in 100 years.

Another flood measure is the provision of a mezzanine as a refuge with its own dedicated window where Paul says, "we'll wait for the boats to arrive and watch the ducks pass by". It also forms part of the studio and sits above the garage. In places the raw prefabricated roofing panels are revealed in the ceiling partly to give texture and relief, partly to suggest different ways of occupying space and also to remind one of the construction.

The combination of flood requirements, low budget and an awkward site led to a specific design response. Together with exploiting a particular construction system this has created a distinctive architecture in time and place—a new vernacular in the truest sense.

SHARING

IMAGINING THE JUST CITY
ALAN POWERS

OPEN YOUTH VENUE
GREYFRIARS HOUSING
MEDICAL RESEARCH COUNCIL
CASTLEFORD TOWN SQUARE
STONELEIGH ROAD
SALVATION ARMY

Open Youth Venue is an innovative and inspiring world for teenagers providing a safe place to explore and share their interests; whether it is making music, climbing, getting a job or health advice or just meeting up, the venue has a wide-range of facilities on offer.

IMAGINING THE JUST CITY
ALAN POWERS

Salvation Army.

We like buildings that represent significant forms of social reinvention. Think of Mary Ward House in Bloomsbury from 1898, a novel mixture of residential college, drop-in teaching space and sports hall, or the Peckham Health Centre of 1935, built around a swimming pool with added library, medical suite and cafe.

These were hybrids of existing building types that sprang from the imagination of their clients, who saw the need for new combinations of existing facilities, and the enabling ability of their architects who gave memorable form to these aspirations and worked beyond the call of professional duty because they shared a belief in the mission. Although neither remains in its original use, their special qualities as places for people are remembered.

It is hard to reconstruct quite how fresh each of these buildings would have seemed when they were new. One imagines the surprise and delight of the original users who, even if not expert in architecture, would have detected an almost cheeky sense of fun in these works rather than the more serious qualities that architectural historians detect there.

Hudson Architects' work at the Salvation Army Citadel in Baddow Road, Chelmsford was much more than just a makeover, although there was a previous building on the site whose footprint is still evident in the main church hall. New functions sit on two sides of it, offering a mix of spaces for different functions and events throughout the week. It is a building with a lot going on architecturally inside as well, and every opportunity has been taken to bring in light from different directions. The layout is simple, but it is full of character, with the use of coloured wall linings and the pleasant sense of being in an airy cabin, which comes as a bonus with the use of the structural laminated timber. The outside of the building has something of the same multiple personality, with different faces appropriate to their conditions: a cinema-like canopy on zinc-clad Baddow Road, turning into a red slice of wall round the corner where, incidentally, the 'Tree of Life' theme cut into the surface echoes the symbolic brick pattern on the end wall of Mary Ward House, while the main road side has become a local landmark with its iridescent 'tower'.

Others have noticed how successfully this design has acted on the perceptions of the American architect and theorist, Robert Venturi in the 1960s about architecture's role in sending signals, an influence the architect is happy to

Salvation Army.

Open Youth Venue.

admit. Venturi's vital purpose was to try to get architects off their high horses of purity and abstraction and closer to the life of the sidewalk. He realised that the vitality of American cities lay precisely in the vulgar commercial signage and joke architecture that purists wished to clean up. Nothing could be more appropriate for a building such as the Citadel, giving a lift to a rather knocked-about street on the edge of the town. For too long, the seriousness of modern architecture demanded that the building was mute, but, appropriately for an organisation where loud music has always been key to the emotional call of salvation, the Chelmsford building sings in several keys but without discord.

The idea of "building the just city" as WH Auden put it in his 1937 poem "Spain", runs through the Chelmsford project and with equal urgency. We have not been as clever or sensitive in making our cities work for people as we should have been in the decades of material progress since the war. Certain sections of the population tend to get left out, especially teenagers. Meeting their needs in a way that is both serious and fun has seldom been attempted with imagination, leaving a disastrous hole in intergenerational sympathy and nurture.

Open Youth Venue is a physical transformation from a rather pompous inter-war bank into another place for loud music—notionally secular but still founded in a Salvationist idea. The combination of functions that the Open serves is particularly original, rather like the inspired idea of Henry Morris, the Director of Education for Cambridgeshire County Council between the wars, who created what he called "Village Colleges" by combining a secondary school with a public library and social centre, opening round the clock to serve the needs of different sections of the community, offering an alternative to the village pub that was more attuned to the needs of the whole family.

At Open, Anthony Hudson's architectural and decorative inventions play off against Edward Boardman's ground bass with real verve. As with his other work, it isn't just a visual display, but one rooted in a sense of how people will use different spaces. Again, as at Chelmsford, there is an understanding of how connected spaces offer both security and reassurance, leading from the large performance hall into the more specific areas. At the Peckham Health Centre, the founders, Doctors Williamson and Pearse, realised that older people, especially women, might feel embarrassed about using the swimming bath, so they provided a

Greyfriars Housing.

Stoneleigh Road.

Castleford Town Square.

cafe overlooking the pool that not only allowed mothers to keep an eye on their children but showed them that other people like themselves were willing to risk the pleasure of a dip. More subtly, the doctors were present on the upper floor so that families could get a check up without the fuss of a formal appointment. Something of this intuitive commonsense has informed Open's catering for the more serious sides of teenage life as well as the raves and gigs, and the different scales of intimacy and privacy seem to fit into the envelope of the site and existing building as if it had been made for them.

These two projects have been highlighted here as a pair showing similar kinds of social invention and re-invention of building types. The others in the pages that follow are closer to convention, such as the Greyfriars Road housing in Norwich, the Stoneleigh Road shared workspace in Haringey and the Medical Research Council building in Cambridge. Even so, each of these is highly particularised in relation to its site and its use, showing a range of surface finishes which are part of the architectural trend of the past 15 years.

The market project at Castleford was a different order of restoring part of a town, in the context of a rather staged combination of regeneration projects, whose achievement could have been greater if there had been a more sustained commitment to completing all aspects of the project. At Castleford, shopping activity had been left, as it nearly always is, to market forces enabled by several generations of submissive planners, but it was in jeopardy in 2008 when the scheme began, and the situation will only have become worse since then. Hudson Architects were chosen to bring the daily covered market back into the pedestrianised main street, planning custom-designed folding market stalls for easy transformation of the space to alternative uses. Anthony Hudson explains that "the most important thing is that the people engage with and respond to the architecture. Just like you need spaces in a house to address complexities of family life the same goes for public buildings. They need not only to be welcoming but feel safe, secure and understandable." This is not even a building in the conventional sense, more a refurnishing of the street and a new floor. The Hudson sense of fun comes across in the coloured swivel chairs, and the practicality in the benches that can easily be unlocked and carried away when the street needs to be opened up for special events. Although the Channel 4 series with Kevin McCloud was based on the idea that architects could save an ailing town centre

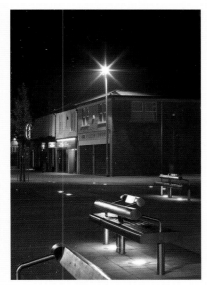

Castleford Town Square.

through the quality of their ideas, it is no discredit to their skills and ingenuity to suggest that more than this is needed, and that the malaise of the economy runs too deep. That said, something is always better than nothing, and the distinctive high quality hardware goes well beyond the normal sticking plaster interventions.

Does regenerating a shopping centre have much in common with a Salvation Army building or a teenage music venue? In one sense, the last two are forms of antidote to the first, providing the elements that are missing from a life of materialism, through directed forms of social activity. Tuning up a street is the most that a designer can normally do to help, but the effort is part of the same desire to understand people's lives in several dimensions and provide the physical setting that can provide some zing at the right volume that is represented by the other projects.

If we could imagine versions of each of the buildings described here placed within easy walking distance of each other, we would have one of the best visions of a better future that architecture is likely to offer us in this difficult decade. Given that two of them are in Norwich, is this set to become a model for Auden's "just city" in our lifetime?

Opposite The angular geometry of the new mezzanine contrasts with the existing classical architecture of arches and vaults along the banking hall aisle. The indentations in the mezzanine balustrade create gathering places.

Right The main banking hall has been transformed into a venue housing events for up to 1,500 people. The introduction of new elements such as the mezzanine creates more space, and the flying 'toblerones' provide dramatic lighting and ideal acoustics.

OPEN YOUTH VENUE

LOCATION: Norwich, UK.
DESCRIPTION: Conversion of Grade II listed building into a state-of-the-art youth venue.
DATE: 2009.

Young people under 18 looking for places to go out in our towns and cities have been treated pretty shabbily. And so they might be found congregating on the street, trying to get into a bar or getting into trouble with alcohol or drugs. The general wish is to move them off the streets but where can they go? The Open Youth Venue offers exactly that: a place that is a haven with a multitude of things a teenager might want to do. It is a pioneering building, the first of its kind in England, and has been the inspiration for many others.

Within the main entrance lobby angular low-level partitions, nicknamed "icebergs" subdivide the space and provide channels for queuing or serving as a waiting or seating area.

At the top of one of the main thoroughfares of Norwich sits a stern-looking Grade II listed former bank. Built of brick with stone dressings it is of Edwardian appearance but was actually built much later in 1929 for the Gurney banking family and designed by the architect Edward Boardman. It was taken over by Barclays before being sold to the Open Trust when the bank finally closed. From the start the Trust involved teenagers who had a say in everything; from what activities should go on inside to furniture, graphics and colour. From an initial wish list, a nightclub for 350, live performance space, climbing wall, cafe, dance studio, workspace and recording studios were chosen. The Trust also offers advisory services to young people on jobs and health, so providing space for this was crucial to the mix and is partly this that makes it different from youth clubs of past years. Spaces used by other youth-focused organisations help pay the rent together with other peripheral uses such as conference facilities and archive storage. The latter occupy the extraordinary bank vaults in the basement, where the country's gold reserves were kept safe during the Second World War. As well as accommodating myriad uses, each activity has to operate either in tandem with others or separately, with the proviso that the core youth space, which occupies what was the central courtyard of the bank, is always available for use by young people.

The building occupies a triangular site bounded on two sides at different levels by the streets, Bank Plain and Castle Meadow. To enable multiple uses a new entrance onto Castle Meadow was created that connects back to the main entrance off Bank Plain. Also off Castle Meadow there is third new, but dedicated, entrance to the nightclub. A fourth new entrance serves the conference centre. The Bank Plain reception area contains 'iceberg' shaped low partitions used for seating, leaning or waiting; intentionally ambiguous in use responding to children's imaginative appropriation of anything that looks interesting. Here teenagers congregate before entering the largest space in the building, the magnificent basilica shaped banking hall now used as the main performance space for up to 1,500 people. To make it work as a venue a number of interventions were

Top Left In contrast to the vibrant hub within, the austere exterior of the original Grade II listed bank site has changed very little.

Bottom left Teenage aesthetics; the youth forum was composed of 12 to 18 year olds and was instrumental in giving direction to the project. One thing they were determined to have was well-designed and practical but fun washrooms.

Right The two new elements that have transformed the banking hall space into the venue are the acoustic baffles and the mezzanine. Their trapezoid forms contrast with the coffered vaulting of the hall.

Opposite Contrasting forms but similar colours: in the banking hall, the gilded Corinthian capitals frame the vaulted apse and contrast dramatically with the golden anodised mesh of the acoustic baffles. Fondly referred to as 'toblerones', these are multi-functioning structures.

Above The nightclub can be independent from the rest of the building through the use of its own private entrance or, for a bigger venue, it can be used in conjunction with the main hall. Robustly detailed walls are clad in galvanised metal sheet and the floor is black stained sprung oak.

made all of which are reversible due to the Grade II listing.

A third of the way along the hall a mezzanine provides space for meetings as well as extra standing and a vantage point for events; its sides are a modern version of a crinkle-crankle wall with pockets for people to gather. All new insertions are visually separated from the existing architectural landscape, contrasting old and new. Angular forms and materials both refers to the bank building and acts as a counterpoint. In some areas this was determined by practical necessity due to the triangular shape of the site, while elsewhere—as in the banking hall—the trapezoid shapes echo the keystone motifs of the classical architecture. The architectural references continue with gold anodised grillage cladding the mezzanine and acoustic baffles reminiscent of gilded Corinthian capitals: the latter being one bit of the original architecture that teenagers seem to warm to. The most dramatic insertions are the acoustic baffles—'toblerone-shaped' flying

objects that seemingly career around the roof space. As well as providing acoustic absorption they incorporate lighting and have an architectural function in articulating routes and views through the building.

The galleries, running the full length of the hall aisles provide further gathering spaces. They lead through an arcade into what was originally an external courtyard to the bank, subsequently built over but now re-opened to the sky. This is the social hub of the venue and has a deliberate outdoor feel. With white wall tiles akin to Victorian lightwells and grass-like green flooring and lamp-posts, it is treated like a street. Containing a cafe the two-storey space has views and access to most of the venue's activities including a games area, media suites, health suite, youth advice rooms and a dance studio. A climbing wall runs the full height of the venue cutting through all the floors and overlooks activities taking place on each.

Right The climbing wall as seen from the social hub and cafe at the centre of the building. Rising from the floor below it runs up to the media and computer areas above.

Opposite The cafe sits in a former courtyard and links to all the main spaces and activities of the building. To the left is the kitchen, and above a bridge connecting the media area to the dance studio. Arched doorways on the rear wall open onto the mezzanine balconies overlooking the main space of the original banking hall.

Running along Castle Meadow are small offices providing home to organisations related to youth services including a dedicated youth health suite. The bank boardrooms, the grandest in the building, sit at the apex of the triangle at ground and first floor levels from which the governor would look on as Norfolk farmers deposited their hard-earned cash. These rooms now form part of a conference centre that can function independently of the venue.

The radical transformation of the venue is in no small part due to the youth forum that played a vital role in encouraging both architects and Trust to be bold and brave. The judicious mixture of restraint and exciting ideas, original architecture and new interventions was only made possible by the shared ambition by all parties to make a great place for young people in the city.

GREYFRIARS HOUSING

LOCATION: Norwich, UK.
DESCRIPTION: New build mixed-use development comprising residential and commercial units.
DATE: 2003.

Opposite Cream tiles used on the courtyard elevations echo the plasterwork of some of Norwich's Medieval and Georgian buildings.

Left The main entrance to the courtyard is off Greyfriars Road and named after the friary that once stood here. The gateway is formed by a seven-storey tower and buildings that wrap around the urban courtyard.

Right The entrance to all houses and flats is off the courtyard encouraging shared use of the space, and reminiscent of the original friary cloisters.

Greyfriars reinterprets Norwich's distinctive urban forms of the courtyard and plain in a housing scheme in the city centre. It shows that more can be made of the parts by giving new pedestrian routes and public space back to the city as well as acknowledging its deep history.

Norwich has a rich tradition of urbanism and housing stemming from the Middle Ages; some of the most interesting were built around courtyards off main streets creating a semi-public world that encourages a sense of identity and shared use. It is also a city with a significant heritage of Medieval buildings now forgotten underground. Most significant are the remains of the many religious buildings that were lost after Henry VIII's Dissolution of the Monasteries. Greyfriars Friary was one such building and its footprint spreads across this site and under adjacent buildings and roads. The project recreates the urban form of courtyard housing as well as making reference to the friary that once dominated the site.

The scheme consists of 130 flats including social housing, shops and offices. The site is just off King Street—once the main road out of Norwich to London—and had been empty and cleared of buildings for years. There is a one-storey drop across the site with archaeological remains of the friary at the lower level. Together with car parking these are over-sailed by an upper deck that relates to the higher levels of the site. The main entrance to the courtyard is at this level, via Greyfriars plain (a plain being another distinctive urban form to Norwich), and is marked by a seven-storey residential tower in grey-black bricks alluding to the flint church

towers that make a significant silhouette on Norwich's skyline. The scheme was built under a 'design and build' contract and the tower top does not reflect the original design.

The courtyard is a semi-public space used by the residents and employs an urban form common to Norwich. It is also a reminder of the cloisters from the demolished friary and a place for quiet contemplation. The buildings have a varied profile: ranging from three to six storeys around the courtyard. The grey-black bricks form a plinth above which upper floors project like the jettied houses of Medieval Norwich. These floors are clad in off-white tiles giving a colour, pattern and texture similar to plasterwork seen on buildings throughout the city. To one side of the court a stepped ramp connects to the lower level and is bounded by a new flint wall marking the line of the original friary precinct wall. This was later omitted. The route runs down to Rose Lane along which shops and offices back onto the housing.

The project is based on a reinterpretation of historic Norwich urban forms, textures and colours, and makes a distinctive contribution to the contemporary street scene while bringing new life to a neglected but important part of the city.

MEDICAL RESEARCH COUNCIL

LOCATION: Chaucer Road, Cambridge, UK.
DESCRIPTION: New build two-storey research and teaching building.
DATE: 2001.

Research into the way the brain works and affects our behaviour has always been an important part of the Medical Research Council's (MRC) activity. By reorganising their Chaucer Road campus and adding new laboratories and teaching space the unit has been able to further extend its research and share its knowledge. The buildings, in their modest way, pay homage to this by combining some visual tricks with practical needs.

Previous page left The south elevation opens onto mature gardens. An external staircase gives access from the first floor lecture theatre and seminar rooms.

Previous page right Detail of the north entrance elevation. The yellow blinkers to the laboratory windows give privacy from passers-by and bring vibrancy to a formerly blank wall.

Bottom left The new two-storey extension has been grafted onto the existing Edwardian house. The house has since been converted for academic use. The new building, housing laboratories and teaching spaces, pays tribute to the larger house.

Bottom right Garden elevation showing yellow walls of the internal tapered corridor protruding at ground floor level.

This particular outpost of the MRC, the Cognitive and Brain Sciences Unit (CBU), has historically researched patterns of thinking. In its first guise as the Applied Psychological Research Unit during the Second World War, scientists investigated how armed combat affected services personnel's behaviour and reasoning as they went about their duties. Personnel were subject to a range of simulated situations and their reaction was observed and recorded. It was all quite hand to mouth with laboratories (testing cubicles) dotted here and there and built ad hoc throughout the building. The cumulative result made for a disorganised jumble of rooms inherited by successive directors. At the same time the focus of research has moved towards more benign aims covering psychology, memory, emotion and language. With modern testing techniques came the need for better laboratories and, with the increasing prestige of the department, came the need of sharing their research requiring seminar rooms and a lecture theatre. This

was the incentive to completely reorganise the campus and provide new accommodation under the new director, William Marslen-Wilson.

A three-storey block, formerly a large Edwardian house, is the centrepiece of the campus and has single-storey 60s brick wing running down one side of the site. These were refurbished and all the old testing laboratories were stripped out: the former now being the social and administrative hub of the unit while the latter accommodates the scientists and PhD students. To the other side of the house a single-storey building was demolished to make way for a new two-storey building for all new laboratories, teaching spaces and technicians.

The new building, despite being two storeys, is treated as single-storey from the front so as to be subservient to the house. A black panelled strip, the vestige of a cornice, brings down the visual height and a full-height glazed entrance creates a visual break to the adjacent building. Like the 1960s wing,

Top The lecture theatre looks into a canopy of trees, setting a contemplative backdrop for teaching, learning and discussion.

Bottom Two views of the tapered corridor that play with perspective. The corridor widens to the garden and so foreshortens the view (above). Towards the north forecourt it narrows and makes it look more distant (below).

a similar coloured brick has been used to match the original building.

All laboratories were re-sited on the ground floor because of the wall mass needed for acoustic separation, and are arranged around tapered corridors for both practical and architectural reasons. The angled walls prevent standing sound waves occurring in both laboratories and passage which would interfere with tests, and the tapered corridor creates false perspective views that play with one's sense of distance: an allusion to the research. Laboratories on the external walls carry variously angled 'blinkers' to each side of the window, creating privacy to volunteers or subjects being tested from passers-by and helping to animate an otherwise blank brick wall.

Lectures can be held when the central building is closed because of the new entrance from

where a generous staircase rises to a first floor foyer, the main lecture theatre and seminar room overlooking the garden. From the garden things look very different: the building clearly reads as two storeys, with the lightweight glazed rooms projecting into the trees with over-sailing *brise-soleil*. These all sit on a sturdy brick base.

With limited means the new building has become both practical and fun to use and plays on our perception of the world. It is all pertinent to the important research going on inside.

CASTLEFORD TOWN SQUARE

LOCATION: Castleford, Yorkshire, UK.
DESCRIPTION: Town centre urban design scheme.
DATE: 2006.

Much has been written on the benefits gained by communities from regenerating their town centres with improved infrastructure and high-quality public spaces. In 2006–2007, television turned its attention to the possibilities of regeneration in Castleford, with the dysfunctional main square as one of the primary focuses. The project had great ambitions for working with the community, but was thwarted by funding issues and lack of local authority commitment. The results were in the end modest, but have fulfilled some part of the ambition by creating a public space that is both practical and a focus for the community.

Previous page left The new town square is a public space used by all ages. Here children enjoy the swivel seats; situated along one side of the square, these seats transform into different groupings depending on the desires of their occupant.

Previous page right The space is brought together as a whole with paving and bench seats defining different areas, all highlighted at night by strategic lighting.

Above The pattern of dark and light granite sets gives scale to the square with light patches identifying the location of bench seats. Within each darker strip there are two alternative positions for the bench; one for events when the square is cleared and they are placed along the top edge, and a default position with the benches distributed across the square.

Opposite top The square cleared for community events; here for the annual Maypole Festival.

Opposite bottom The colours of the swivel seats are those of the Castleford Tigers rugby league team.

Known as "Kevin McCloud and the Big Town Plan", the project was initiated by Channel 4 in partnership with Wakefield Council. For Channel 4 it was to be a 'fly on the wall' documentary about the regeneration of a small Yorkshire town while the council would see the economic and social benefits as a result. Castleford exhibited all the problems of a failing town centre due to loss of jobs and general economic paralysis. It had suffered, like other Yorkshire communities, from the closure of coal mines from the 1970s onwards. Subsequently its economy had been further dented by the growth of out-of-town shopping centres that have more or less torn the town's heart out. Nevertheless, Castleford has a strong identity: a wealth of history stemming back to Roman times that blossomed in the Industrial Revolution, the popular Castleford Tigers rugby team, and pride in alumni such as the sculptor Henry Moore. It is a heritage and identity that the community wanted to celebrate, focusing on the town square as a stage for public events throughout the year. But there was a problem: the square had been designed as an undulating surface giving more priority to water drainage than human

activity. On top of this few of the shops around the square offered street activity and an erratic and confusing clutter of street furniture and trees made the space even more problematic for public events.

Like all the Castleford projects this went out to a design competition. This scheme proposed bringing life back to the square with cafes, market, public events and places to stop, sit and chat. Combined with interpreting the town's heritage this all struck a cord with the community and the proposal was chosen.

An element included re-establishing a daily market on the High Street that runs into the square. While encouraging stalls back on to the main street, the council also needed them to be easily dismountable so they were designed as a series of permanently sited large folding umbrellas that took up little space when not in use. Sadly, although stallholders enthusiastically took up the idea, the council gave insufficient resources and commitment to properly prototype the idea, which was never taken any further.

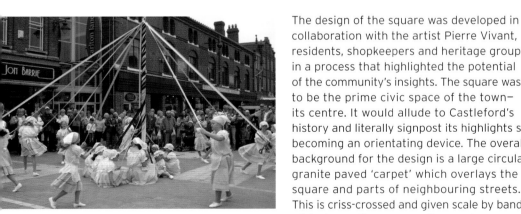

The design of the square was developed in collaboration with the artist Pierre Vivant, residents, shopkeepers and heritage groups in a process that highlighted the potential of the community's insights. The square was to be the prime civic space of the town— its centre. It would allude to Castleford's history and literally signpost its highlights so becoming an orientating device. The overall background for the design is a large circular granite paved 'carpet' which overlays the square and parts of neighbouring streets. This is criss-crossed and given scale by bands of dark granite representing coal seams. Across the circle's diameter, facing south, is a strip of contrasting paving (originally devised as a graphic time-line representing the town's history) on which individual seats are placed in groups to encourage people to congregate and chat. The seats themselves are specifically designed to rotate to different positions for different groupings—so allowing the arrangements to change but also being fun for children to play with; they are also in the colours of Castleford Tigers rugby team. The remainder of the square can inter-change between an open stage for events, such as

Maypole dancing or occasional large markets when all the benches are located against the paved strip, or a default position with benches dotted around the square. It allows the whole square to be colonised by the town.

In the event Vivant's central focus was not built due to lack of funding. What remains works well and provides space for community events, markets and day-to-day life. However it could have been much more; local people, once engaged in the process, were advocates of radical change. It is a shame the council was uncommitted and failed to share the enthusiasm of locals for whom, in the end, this project was all about.

STONELEIGH ROAD

LOCATION: Tottenham, North London, UK.
DESCRIPTION: New build managed office.
DATE: 2007.

Haringey Council commissioned Stoneleigh Road as part of an inner city regeneration initiative. Providing managed workspace to encourage new businesses to set up in a low energy building, it is a modest yet flagship development with a strong community focus.

Previous page left Now a local landmark the pink ventilation towers herald the building, seen here from the street market on Tottenham High Road.

Previous page right Offices are arranged on the north and east sides of the building to avoid solar gain. The window sizes are determined by internal daylight requirements.

Below Anti-graffiti paint on blockwork provides a robust base around the building. Above horizontal timber panels clad the timber frame in a brickwork pattern.

The site was a disused council building depot that had various nefarious uses in a part of Tottenham that had been neglected over the years. However it is well located next to a street market on the edge of a busy thoroughfare running from Tottenham High Road to housing estates in the Haringey hinterland.

The project began by consulting the local community on how the building related to the existing streetscape. Two options proposed a public square or a street with internal courtyard, with the square the early favourite as it offered potential for open air events. However, after extensive discussions with locals it was clear that the street layout would offer a more pleasant, successful and safe environment in the Tottenham context. This

was adopted and it works, demonstrating the power of collective wisdom.

The building has streets on three frontages with the entrance placed on the newly created thoroughfare running from the high street, via the street market, to housing beyond. It has an 'L-shaped' footprint enclosing a south-facing courtyard, onto which all the circulation spaces face. A range of different sized offices and meeting rooms wrap around the north and east sides. This approach ensures that the offices are not subject to overheating and their environment can be managed passively using natural ventilation. This is the purpose of the pink cowls that pepper the top of the building, connecting to vertical full-height ducts serving each office

Circulation spaces are on the west and
south elevations overlooking a courtyard.
These sides of the building are clad in
translucent polycarbonate panels and
windows are interspersed to frame
outward views and provide ventilation.

Right Timber laminated posts create an internal colonnade along circulation spaces. These areas are subtly lit by polycarbonate panels intermixed with full height windows, which combined release a dramatic impression of light and shadow.

Opposite At night the building glows. Shadows and colours from the interior are refracted through the polycarbonate panels, bringing the building to life and giving a sense of openness and activity within the community.

enabling natural stack ventilation while at the same time creating a distinctive identity for the building and the area. The office windows give the optimum amount of natural light with operable louvers to control incoming air. To further reduce heating loads and improve the environmental performance of the building the ceilings are clad in a cement board that provides thermal mass.

Horizontal solid faced timber panels, riveted to the structural frame, clad the office elevations. In contrast the remaining elevations, which relate to circulation spaces, are cloaked with translucent multi-walled polycarbonate

sheet punctured by full-height windows. This animates the building with occupants' shadows moving behind and, at night, acts like a lantern. The circulation spaces are imbued with subtle natural light reducing the need for artificial and work as a stabilising environmental buffer to the offices.

The building had to be very robust for the area. Around the exposed perimeter of the building the ground floor has a masonry base rendered and painted in anti-graffiti paint. Used on such a large scale this has been effective and forms a black rusticated plinth. However the main construction is timber prefabricated panels with

a glulam frame to the circulation spaces on the courtyard side. This ensured a quick, economic and energy efficient build. To complement the market a cafe was planned to one side of the courtyard opening on to the street but this was later dropped due to lack of finance.

On completion the offices were quickly occupied and the pink towers have become a local landmark. The wisdom of the locals has been borne out in how the building relates to public space and it has also been robust enough to deal with life in an often tough neighbourhood.

SALVATION ARMY

LOCATION: Chelmsford, Baddow Road, UK.
DESCRIPTION: New build Salvation Army Citadel.
DATE: 2009.

The Salvation Army has a long tradition of commissioning buildings for local churches and communities known as "corps buildings". Historically they consisted simply of a large worship hall but with the expansion of activities and widening of the Army's mission in the community, they have become more complex buildings to meet the needs of families, youth and the elderly. The new Chelmsford Corps building arose out of those greater demands and consideration of how they fit into their neighbourhoods.

Previous page left The worship hall is the focus of the building providing space for up to 300 people. Primarily for services it is also used by the local community for numerous events such as meetings, weddings and get-togethers.

Previous page right The Salvation Army Corps Citadel has become a landmark building in Chelmsford with its distinctive prismatic tower.

Top The south side of the building faces the hostile environment of a dual carriageway with crash barriers and no pavements. The simple form, clad in zinc shingles with an eye-catching tower, gives a powerful dynamic to an otherwise bland and disheartening landscape.

Bottom The north entrance opens onto Baddow Road with glazed frontage and domestic scale treatment. An open courtyard is to the right and a canopy over-sails the entrance area.

Left Highly visible from Baddow Road (left), the foyer is a welcoming vision for all passing by. Encouraged and invited to enter and use the building as much as possible, people are offered free tea and coffee from the cafe. Off the foyer are all the main spaces of the building; to the right the worship hall and beneath the balcony are rooms of varying size for use by the community.

Right The cafe servery leads to the various community rooms used by all ages. Offices are above, at first floor level, where a balcony runs alongside and overlooks the entrance.

There were many reasons why the 1960s brick building previously on the site was unsuitable: not only was the accommodation inadequate and unworkable, it was un-insulated and freezing in winter, the services were on their last legs and it was becoming increasingly unloved. It also exhibited many of the urban failings of 1960s architecture becalmed on a sea of car parking with no physical relationship to its neighbours. With some cash in the bank the Chelmsford Corps saw an opportunity to have a new, welcoming and dynamic building on the site that would provide a new worship hall and better facilities for the community.

The site is bounded on the southern side by a busy dual carriageway (another unfortunate legacy of the 1960s) and Baddow Road to the north—the once historic high street since severed by highways. Happily, the street is being reclaimed as the main pedestrian

thoroughfare into the town centre. The building's glazed front responds to this, opening onto Baddow Road with views into the foyer and coffee area encouraging as many people as possible to drop in, have a chat and participate in the activities. From the double-height generous foyer all public parts of the building can be seen and easily understood; this is of crucial importance for a public space if people are to be made to feel welcome. The reception and coffee areas are highlighted by coloured panelling and, other than where linings are needed for functional reasons (acoustic or concealing services), the natural finish of the timber wall and ceiling construction have been left exposed.

The main worship hall for 350 people is prominently located directly in line with the main entrance with a raised dais for the minister on the same axis. The hall is

On axis with the main entrance, the worship hall receives pride of place. The cross-laminated timber panels used in construction are left exposed, apart from the acoustic treatment on the sidewalls. Clerestory windows light the space but can also behave as blackouts for certain events.

a wonderful airy space and, like the rest of the building, is simply constructed using cross-laminated timber panels (basically very thick plywood) from Austria. These are extraordinarily versatile and allowed the main structure to go up in three weeks, considerably shortening the build time and consequently the overall cost. But it is in the roof where its structural qualities can be seen to the best effect. The roof has no trusses or cross beams, and relies only on the in-plane stiffness of the panels and steel ties to resist spreading forces. The butterfly shape acts as a diaphragm allowing the high-level clerestory lights. The hall needed to be acoustically sealed and air-conditioned because of the dual carriageway nearby, and air is provided through washable canvas 'socks' which run down each side of the hall providing a visual cap to the acoustic linings below. These are arranged in a chequerboard

pattern in the principal colours of the Salvation Army.

To one side of the foyer, past reception and coffee areas that provide activity and surveillance, is further accommodation for the wide range of activities and events that the Chelmsford Corps provides for toddlers, youth, the elderly and families. The larger hall is kitted out for sports, such as five-a-side football, but also is used for lunches, evening events and playgroups. Two single-storey sub-dividable rooms cater for smaller groups and events for children or elderly people in comfortable, more domestic surroundings. Sandwiched in between these rooms is a kitchen that serves all these spaces via hatches. Running alongside the rooms is a courtyard—originally to allow for further expansion as funds permitted and now a most useful and unexpectedly successful space containing an outside all-weather play area that

Top The inverted 'butterfly' roof form with clerestory windows is an extremely efficient way of constructing a large span space; used here over the worship halls and foyer. The north zinc-clad face of the tower is a single plank of timber displaying a cut out symbol of the cross.

Bottom The courtyard, originally left empty for future expansion, has become one of the most popular areas in the building providing play space and a venue for outside events.

Opposite The east elevation onto Goldlay Road is a vast billboard; depicting the 'Tree of Life' and verses from the Bible it proclaims the mission of the Salvation Army.

Left Verses and branches of the 'Tree' are routed into the cladding panels like a vast circuit-board.

Right A prayer room doubling up as a meeting room sits on the intersection of Goldlay Road and Baddow Road. Inside at high level a second cross is a beacon at night.

is constantly in demand. Overseeing the foyer at first-floor level are offices for the minister.

The building is designed with shallow pitched bays to suit the panels creating a varied yet economical roof profile. On Baddow Road this has been adapted to the rhythm and scale of other buildings on this frontage. Along the dual carriageway the building needs to be understood in a car, passing at speed so here the building is a bold outline and is heralded by a landmark tower. Made out of

one 13 metre panel (the longest that could be transported) the tower is clad in reflective film that changes colour depending on your viewpoint and a cross magically appears and disappears. Driving at speed the tower goes through all colours of the rainbow, giving the Salvation Army the presence they wanted and, at one point, a suitably Biblical burning fiery bush. The zinc shingles that clad both this and the Baddow Road frontage visually encapsulate the building framing the two end elevations: the side street, Goldlay Road, and

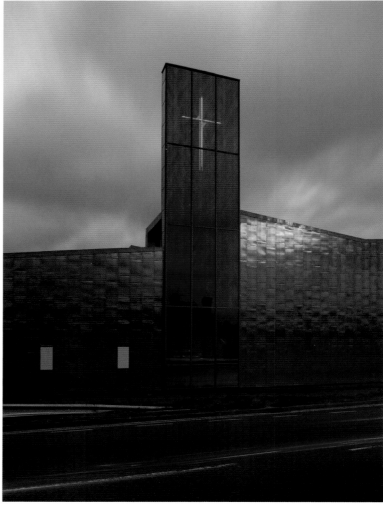

The tower is transformed by varying light and different viewing points. When passing at speed, reflections move across every colour of the rainbow and throw dramatic shafts of coloured light across the road. At night the cross is illuminated from within the structure.

secondly the internal courtyard. Both these have coloured cementitious panels riveted to the structure; the courtyard in yellows and greens reflecting the natural world, whilst the Goldlay Street elevation is a vast billboard resembling the huge signs that the Salvation Army used to paint on the blank sides of their buildings. In this case the image is a 'Tree of Life' with Biblical phrases inscribed into the panels: a muted reference to Victor Hugo's view of cathedrals being a physical manifestation of the Bible.

Major Jones, the minister, sums the building up. "We wanted this to be an accessible place.

It's not a monument on a hill, or an ornament. The great cathedrals are magnificent, but you might not want to have a cup of coffee in them. We want to get back to the Salvation Army and the church as the centre of the community. That's what this is—a community space. It's just a series of boxes but very cleverly done and known locally as the Marmite building—you either love it, or hate it. One fellow said: 'Ah, you've bought a site in Baddow Road'. 'No,' we said, 'we've been here 30 years, and you've never noticed the original building. But now you do!'"

DRAWINGS

BAGGY HOUSE
LIGHT HOUSE
DROP HOUSE
PUSHPANJALI
BAVENT HOUSE
QUAKER AND HALL BARNS
FEERING BURY BARN
ALPES-MARITIMES
56 STOREY'S WAY
CHANTRY FARM
CEDAR HOUSE
OPEN YOUTH VENUE
GREYFRIARS HOUSING
MEDICAL RESEARCH COUNCIL
STONELEIGH ROAD
SALVATION ARMY

BAGGY HOUSE

SITE PLAN

1 Baggy House
2 Driveway
3 Coastal Path
4 Garden
5 Baggy Pool

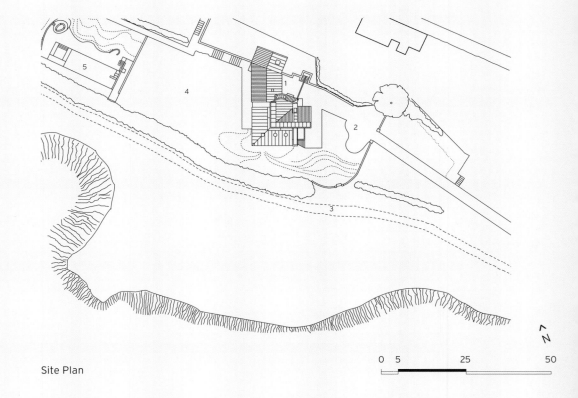

Site Plan

SECTION AA

1 Living
2 Dining
3 Playroom
4 Bedroom

Section AA

SECTION BB

1 Entrance Hall
2 Kitchen
3 Walkway

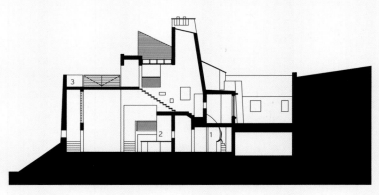

Section BB

SECOND FLOOR

1 Bedroom
2 Bathroom
3 Walkway
4 Terrace

FIRST FLOOR

1 Living
2 Dining
3 Kitchen
4 Sea Room
5 Landing
6 Bedroom
7 Sauna
8 Steam Room
9 Terrace
10 Courtyard Garden

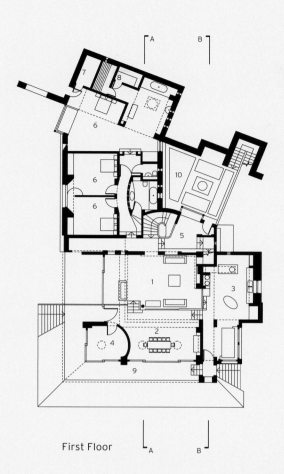

First Floor

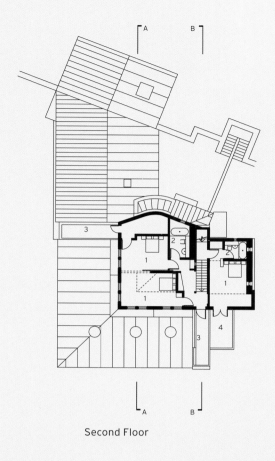

Second Floor

GROUND FLOOR

1 Entrance Hall
2 Garage
3 Kitchen
4 Utility
5 Dining
6 Sea Room
7 Playroom
8 Gym
9 Study
10 Terrace

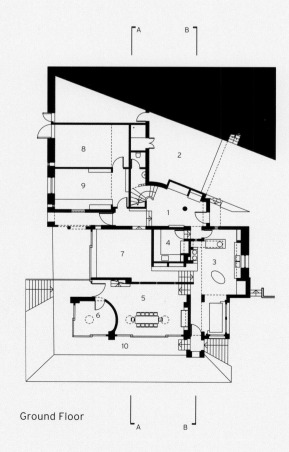

Ground Floor

LIGHT HOUSE

SITE PLAN

1 Light House
2 Stoneyfield Bank
3 Crich Lane
4 Neighbouring House

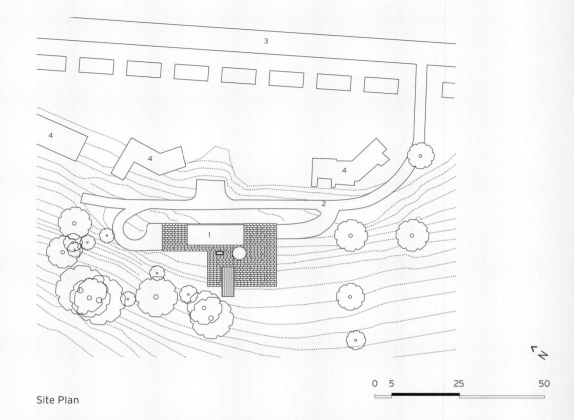

Site Plan

0 5   25   50

SECTIONS

1   Forecourt
2   Master Bathroom
3   Laundry
4   Sun Lounge
5   Study Cabin
6   Living
7   Balcony
8   Bedroom
9   Hall
10 Courtyard

Section AA

Section BB

ROOF PLAN

1   Study Cabin
2   Void (above Sun Lounge)
3   Plant
4   Forecourt (below)

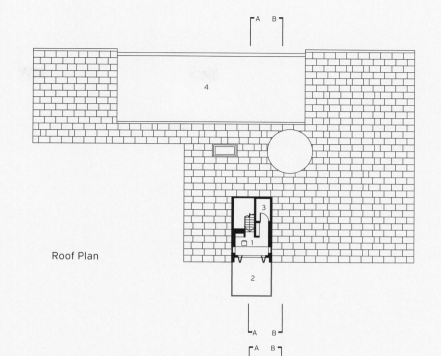

Roof Plan

UPPER GROUND FLOOR

1   Dining
2   Living
3   Kitchen
4   Utility
5   WC
6   Master Bedroom
7   Master Bathroom
8   Sun Lounge
9   Balcony
10 Pool
11 Forecourt
12 Garage

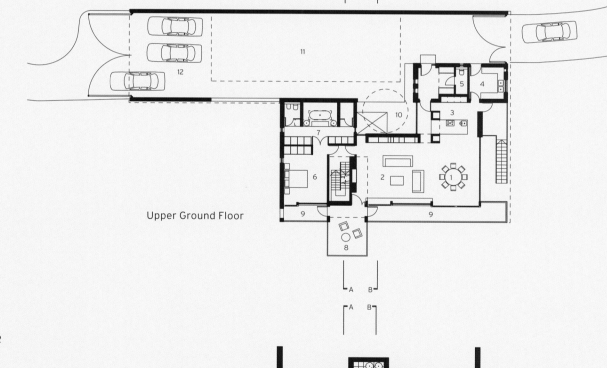

Upper Ground Floor

LOWER GROUND FLOOR

1   Hall
2   Bedroom
3   Bathroom
4   Laundry
5   Store
6   Courtyard

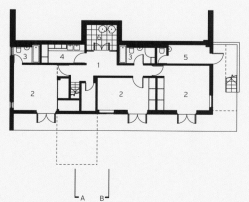

Lower Ground Floor

0 1   5   10

DROP HOUSE

SITE PLAN

1 Drop House
2 Driveway
3 Lawn
4 Coopers Lane Road
5 Neighbouring House
6 Woodland

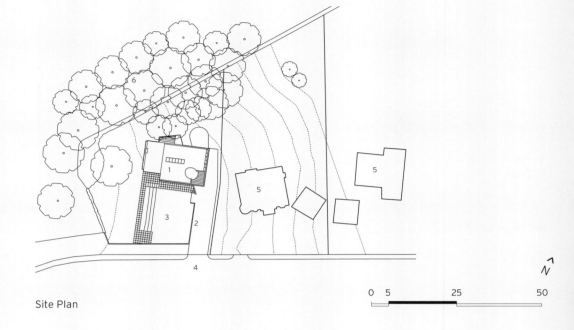

Site Plan

0 5   25   50

SECTIONS

1 Undercroft
2 Entrance Hall
3 Living
4 Main Bedroom
5 Bedroom
6 Gallery
7 Study
8 Study Terrace
9 Kitchen

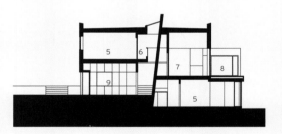

Section AA

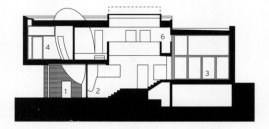

Section BB

FIRST FLOOR

1 Master Bedroom
2 Master Bathroom
3 WC
4 Dressing Room
5 Bedroom Terrace
6 Bedroom
7 Bathroom
8 Gallery
9 Store

UPPER GROUND FLOOR

1 Dining
2 Kitchen
3 Utility
4 Living
5 Study
6 AV Room
7 Sloping Stair Wall
8 External Terrace

LOWER GROUND FLOOR

1 Undercroft
2 Garage
3 Entrance Hall
4 Guest Bedroom
5 Guest Bathroom
6 Store
7 Main Store

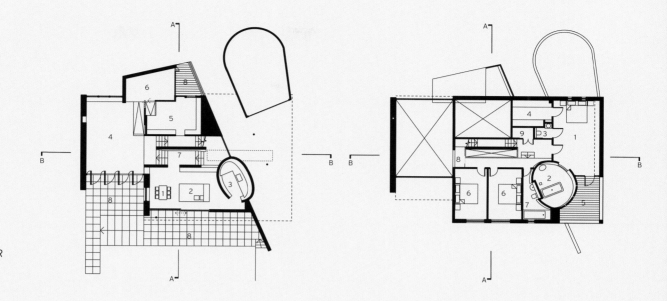

Upper Ground Floor

First Floor

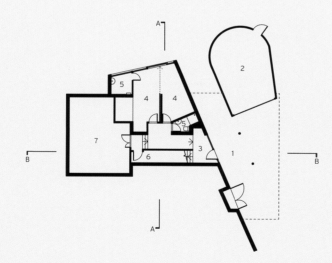

Lower Ground Floor

PUSHPANJALI

SITE PLAN

1 Delhi House
2 Temple
3 Pool Building

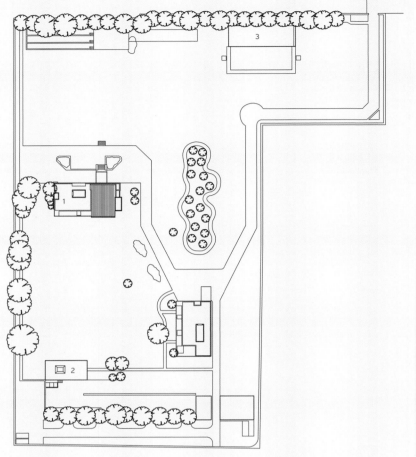

Site Plan

SECTIONS

1 Store Room
2 Living Room
3 Courtyard
4 Kitchen
5 Bathroom
6 Open Shower
7 Wardrobe

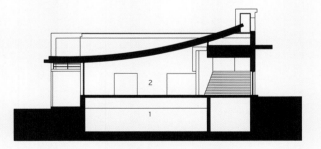

Section AA

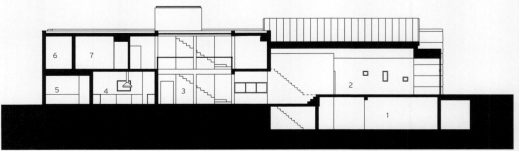

Section BB

FIRST FLOOR

1   Landing
2   Study
3   Bedroom 1
4   Bathroom 1
5   Open Shower
6   Wardrobe
7   Bedroom 2
8   Bathroom 2
9   Terrace

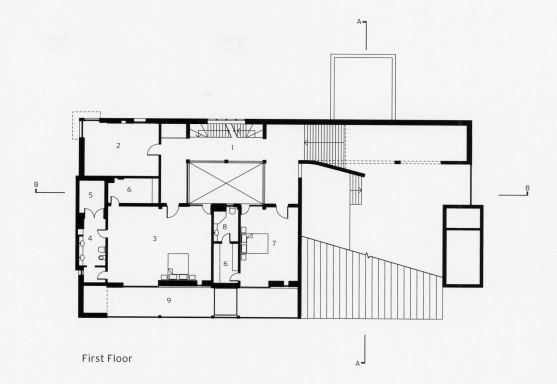

First Floor

GROUND FLOOR

1   Entrance Hall
2   Living Room
3   Small Living Room
4   WC
5   Bar
6   Dining Room
7   Hall
8   Kitchen
9   Pantry
10 Bathroom 3
11 Bedroom 3
12 Wardrobe
13 Courtyard
14 Lower Terrace

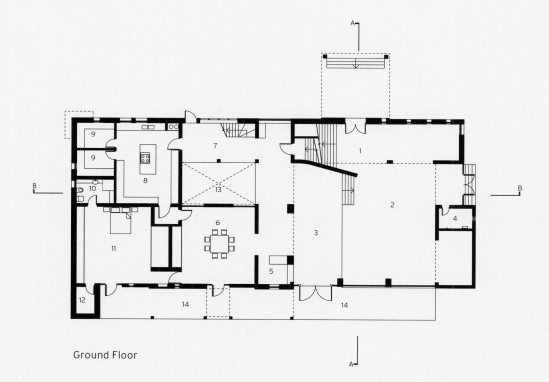

Ground Floor

N

BAVENT HOUSE

SITE PLAN

1   Bavent House
2   Driveway
3   Garden
4   Access Road
5   Derelict Farmhouse

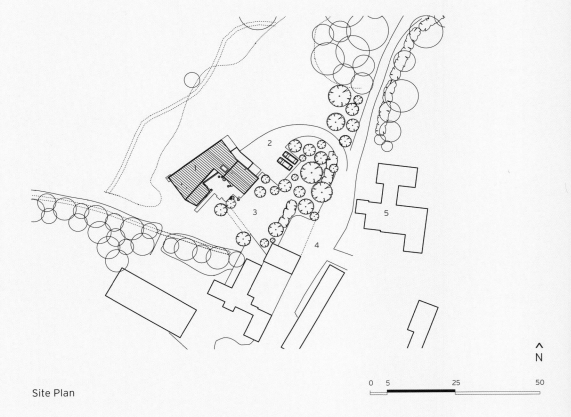

Site Plan

SECTIONS

1   Bridge
2   Living Room
3   Dining Room
4   Kitchen
5   Master Bedroom
6   Bedroom

Section AA

Section BB

MEZZANINE

1 Mezzanine
2 Storage

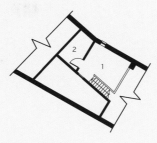

Mezzanine

FIRST FLOOR

1 Master Bedroom
2 Master En suite
3 Bedroom
4 En Suite
5 Landing
6 Bridge
7 Bathroom

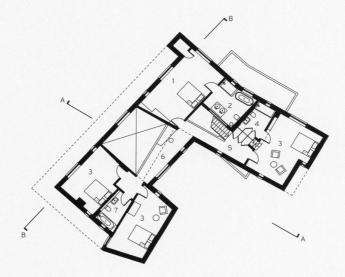

First Floor

GROUND FLOOR

1 Living Room
2 Dining Room
3 Kitchen
4 Hallway
5 WC
6 Snug
7 Utility
8 Lobby
9 Services
10 Dustbins
11 Carport
12 Terrace
13 Decking

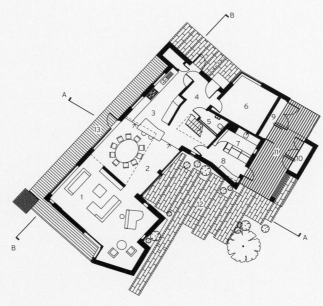

Ground Floor

QUAKER AND HALL BARNS

SITE PLAN

1 Quaker Barn
2 Hall Barn
3 House Garden
4 Parking
5 Terrace
6 Barn Gardens
7 Quaker Hall

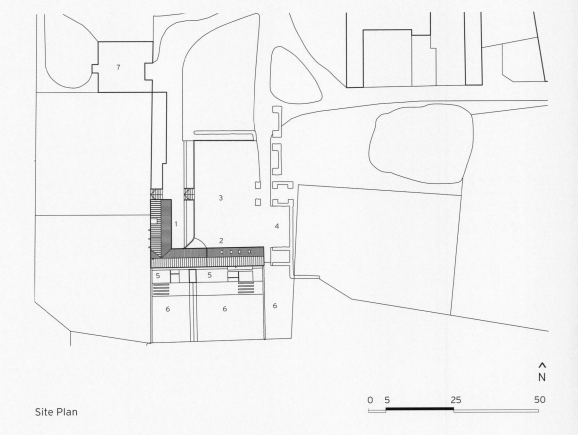

Site Plan

SECTION AA

1 Living
2 Bridge over Void

Section AA

SECTION BB

1 Hall
2 Living
3 Dining
4 Kitchen
5 Bedroom
6 Bridge over Void
7 Store

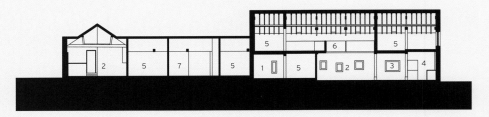

Section BB

GROUND/FIRST FLOOR

1   Covered Entrance
2   Hall
3   Living
4   Dining
5   Kitchen
6   WC/Shower Room
7   Utility
8   Bedroom
9   En suite Bathroom
10 Bridge over Void
11 Store
12 Courtyard
13 Void

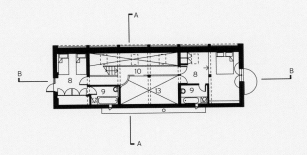

First Floor

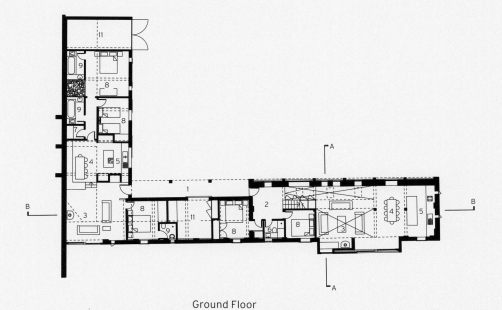

Ground Floor

FEERING BURY BARN

SITE PLAN

1 Driveway
2 Hardstanding
3 Barn
4 Studio and Workshop
  Accommodation
5 Corrugated Silos
6 Woodchip Boiler
7 Woodship Store
8 Open Sided Barn

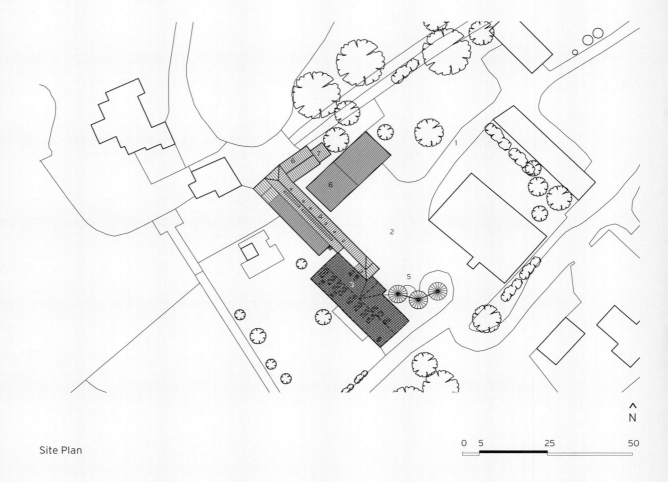

Site Plan

SECTIONS

1 Entrance Lobby
2 Living
3 Utility
4 Metal Workshop
5 Wood Workshop
6 Covered Courtyard
7 South Terrace

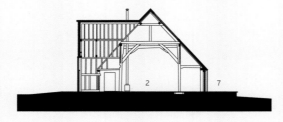

Section AA

Section BB

FIRST FLOOR

1 Master Bedroom
2 Master Bathroom
3 Glazed Screen
4 Void over Kitchen
   and Living
5 Void over Workshop
6 Silos
7 Open Sided
   Dutch Barn

GROUND FLOOR

1 Entrance Lobby
2 Kitchen
3 Living
4 Library
5 Bedroom
6 Ensuite Bathroom
7 Laundry
8 Utility
9 WC
10 Workshop
11 Metal Workshop
12 Wood Workshop
13 Store Room
14 Boiler
15 Wood Chip Store
16 Open Sided
    Dutch Barn
17 Silo
18 Covered Courtyard
19 Courtyard
20 South Terrace

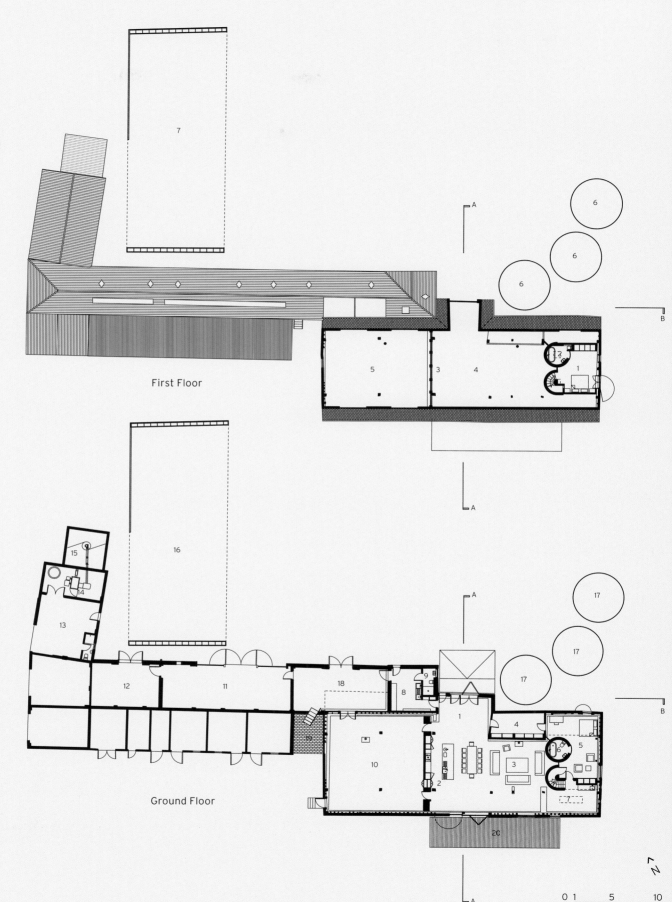

First Floor

Ground Floor

0 1   5   10

ALPES-MARITIMES

SITE PLAN

1   Main House
2   Terrace
3   Garden
4   Swimming Pool
5   Garage

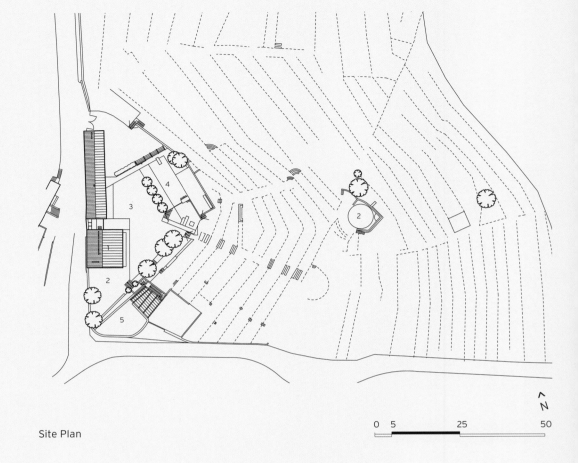

Site Plan

0   5   25   50

SECTIONS

1   Living 1
2   Dining Area/Terrace
3   Kitchen
4   Corridor
5   Game Room
6   Bedroom
7   Office
8   Walkway
9   Bathroom

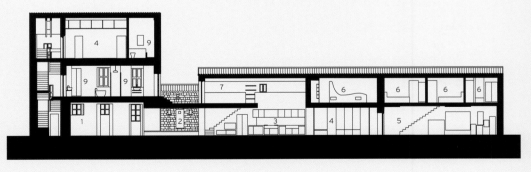

Section AA

Section BB

SECOND FLOOR

1   Bedroom
2   Bathrom

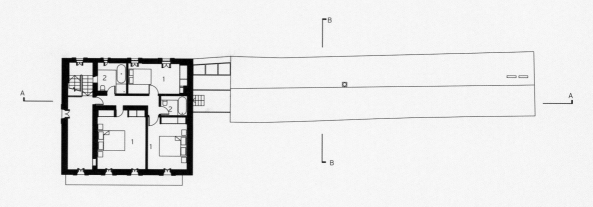

Second Floor

FIRST FLOOR

1   Office
2   Bedroom
3   Walkway
4   WC
5   Wardrobe
6   Bathroom
7   Landing

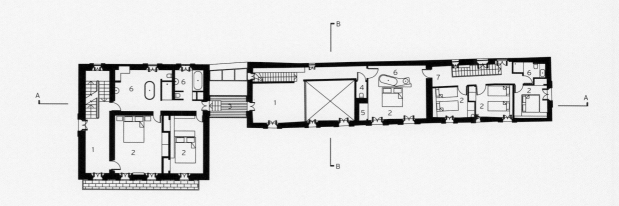

First Floor

GROUND FLOOR

1   Dining Area/Veranda
2   Living 1
3   Main Living Room
4   WC
5   Kitchen
6   Bathroom
7   Utility Room
8   Games Room

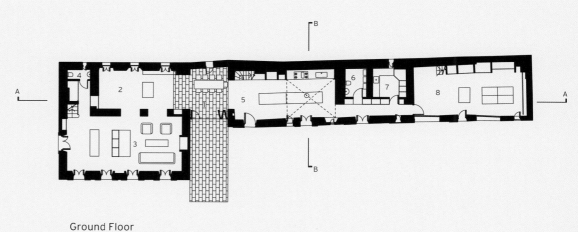

Ground Floor

0   1   5   10

56 STOREY'S WAY

SITE PLAN

1 Extension
2 Existing House
3 Rear Garden
4 Storey's Way
5 Tennis Courts

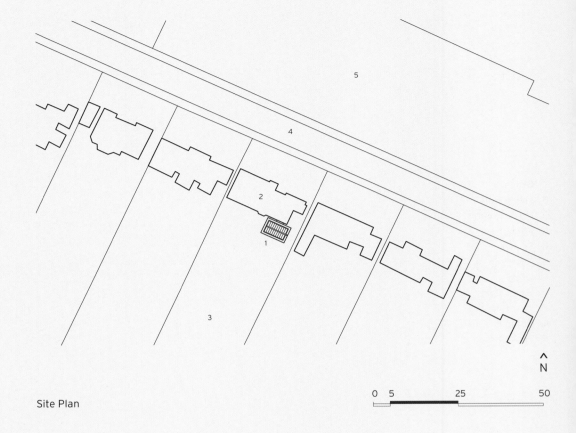

Site Plan

SECTIONS

1 Garden Room
2 Glass Link
3 Kitchen to existing house
4 Access to rear garden
5 Rear garden

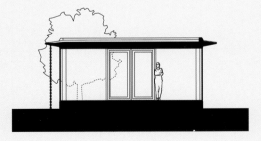

Section AA

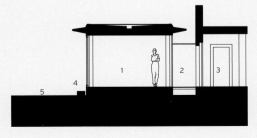

Section BB

GROUND FLOOR

Extension

1 Garden Room
2 Glass Link
3 Access to Rear Garden

Existing House

4 Front Entrance
5 Staircase
6 Hall
7 Office
8 Living Room
9 Music Room
10 Kitchen
11 Scullery
12 Pantry
13 Coats
14 Boiler Room
15 Rear Entrance
16 Garage
17 Rear Garden

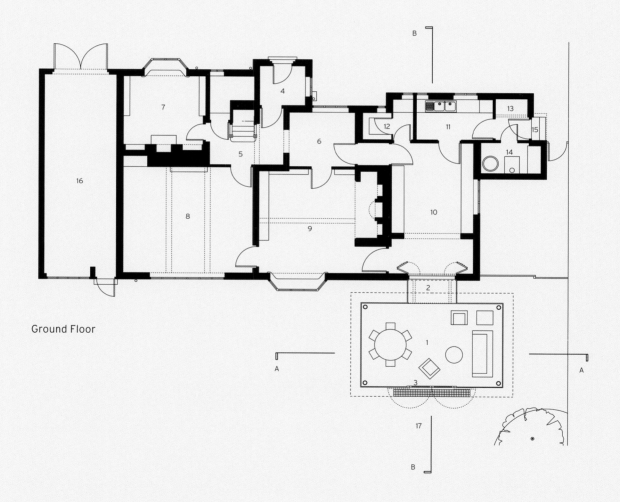

Ground Floor

CHANTRY FARM

SITE PLAN

1   Chantry Farm
2   Cart Barn
3   Church
4   Neighbouring Barns

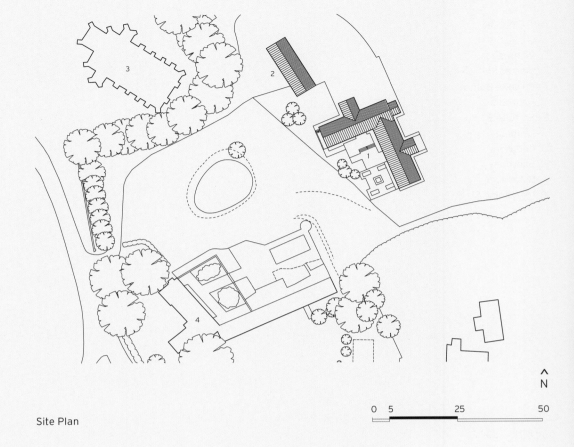

Site Plan

SECTION AA

1   Hall
2   Dining Room
3   Living Room
4   Snug
5   Mezzanine Study
6   Bedroom 4
7   Bedroom 2

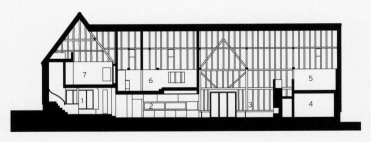

Section AA

SECTION BB

1   Hall
2   Dining Area
3   Walkaway

Section BB

FIRST FLOOR

1 Walkway
2 Master Bedroom
3 En suite Bathroom
4 Bedroom 2
5 En suite 2
6 Landing
7 Bedroom 3
8 Bedroom 4
9 Bathroom
10 Mezzanine Study

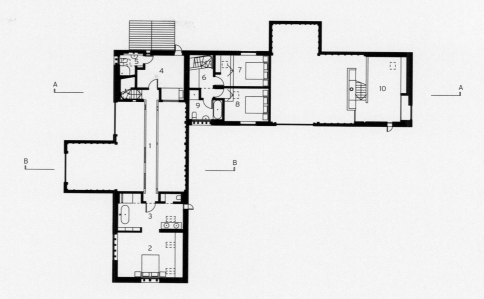

First Floor

GROUND FLOOR

1 Hall
2 WC
3 Kitchen
4 Family Dining
5 Cupboard
6 Bedroom 1
7 En suite 1
8 Utility Room
9 DIning Room
10 Living Room
11 Snug

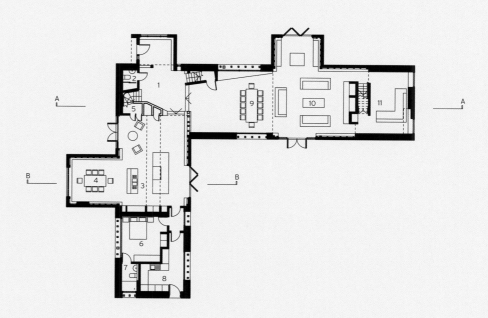

Ground Floor

CEDAR HOUSE

SITE PLAN

1 Cedar House
2 Garage
3 River Wensum
4 Garden
5 Orchard
6 Mill

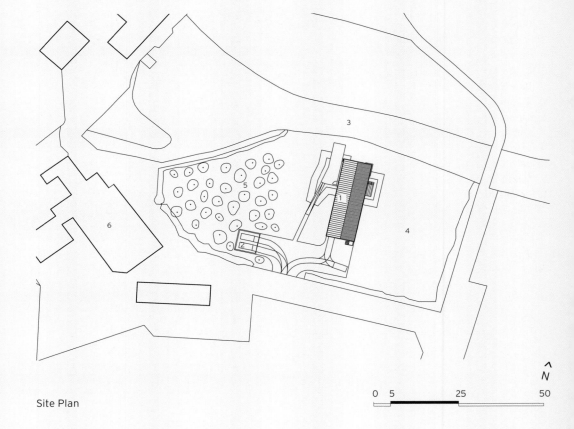

Site Plan

0 5   25   50

N

SECTIONS

1 Living
2 Kitchen
3 Bedroom
4 Dark Room
5 Studio
6 External Deck

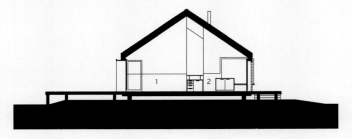

Section AA

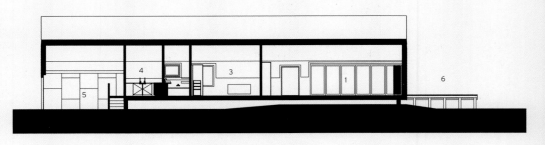

Section BB

GROUND FLOOR

1 Living
2 Dining
3 Kitchen
4 Bedroom
5 Office
6 Dark Room
7 Studio
8 Garage/Mezzanine
  (above)
9 External Deck
10 Bathrooms/WC
11 Mezzanine
12 Double-height
   Space to Studio

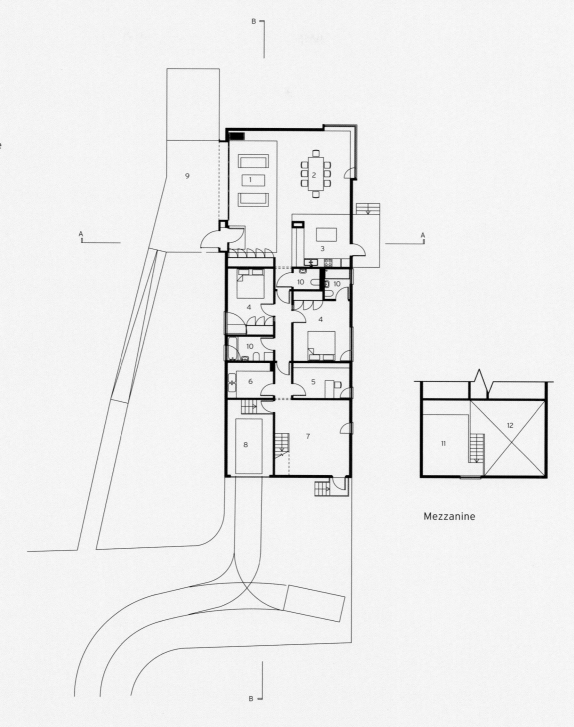

Ground Floor

Mezzanine

0 1   5   10

OPEN YOUTH VENUE

SITE PLAN

1 Open Youth Venue
2 Glazed Roof
3 Courtyard
4 Bank Plain
5 Castle Meadow
6 Agricultural Hall Plain
7 Upper King Street

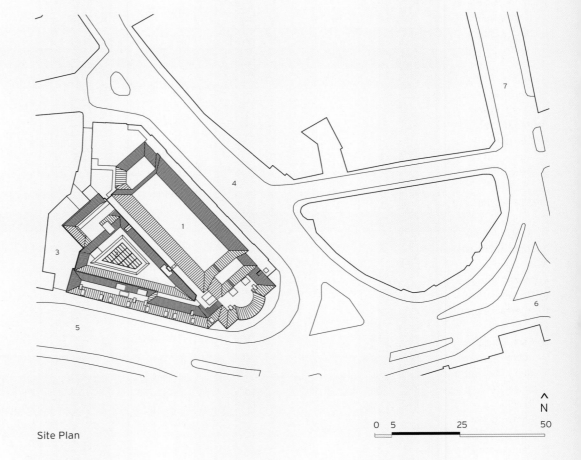

Site Plan

SECTION AA

1 Main Hall
2 Multi-purpose Wall
3 Servery
4 Cafe
5 Rear Entrance
6 Health Clinic Waiting Room
7 Plant
8 Rooflight

Section AA

SECTION BB

1 Offices
2 Conference
3 Main Hall Event Venue
4 Mezzanine
5 Agency Offices
6 Acoustic Baffles

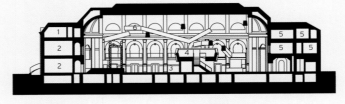

Section BB

SECOND FLOOR

1   Accoustic Baffles
    (above Hall)
2   Dance Studio
3   Agency Offices
4   Reading Area
5   Void
6   Work and Media
7   Climbing Wall
8   Health Suite
9   Consulting Rooms
10 Agency Offices
11 Offices

FIRST FLOOR

1   Gantry (above Stage)
2   Void (above Main Hall)
3   Mezzanine
4   Mezzanine Walkway
5   Conference Kitchen
6   Agency Offices
7   Cafe
8   Cafe Kitchen
9   Lobby
10 Night Club Entrance
11 Entrance
12 Play
13 Climbing Wall
14 Agency Offices
15 Conference Meeting Room

GROUND FLOOR

1   Stage
2   Main Hall
3   Store
4   Meeting Room
5   Cloaks
6   Lobby
7   Reception
8   Office
9   Lobby
10 Bar
11 Venue WCs
12 Night Club WCs
13 Cloakroom
14 Pay
15 Medical
16 Void (below New Conference)
17 Bar
18 Night Club
19 Climbing Wall
20 Green Rooms
21 Conference Rooms
22 Recording Studios

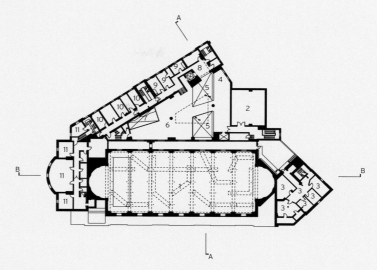

Second Floor

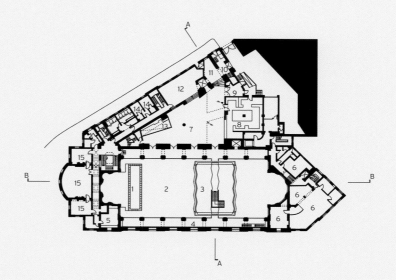

First Floor

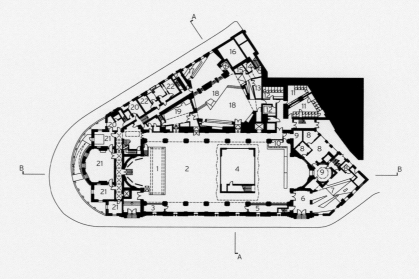

Ground Floor

0   5   10   25

GREYFRIARS HOUSING

SITE PLAN

1   Greyfriars Lane
2   Maidstone Road
3   Rose Lane
4   Courtyard
5   Tower
6   Residential
7   Commercial

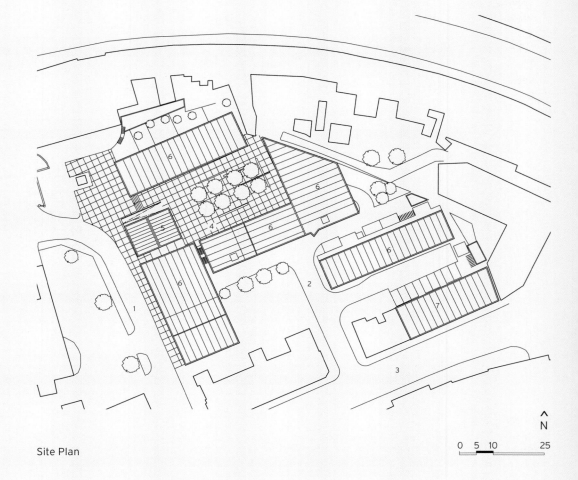

Site Plan

0 5 10   25

^
N

SECTIONS

1   Courtyard
2   Tower
3   Residential

Section AA

Section BB

TYPICAL FLOOR PLAN

1 Greyfriars Lane
2 Maidstone Road
3 Rose Lane
4 Courtyard
5 Tower
6 Residential
7 Commercial

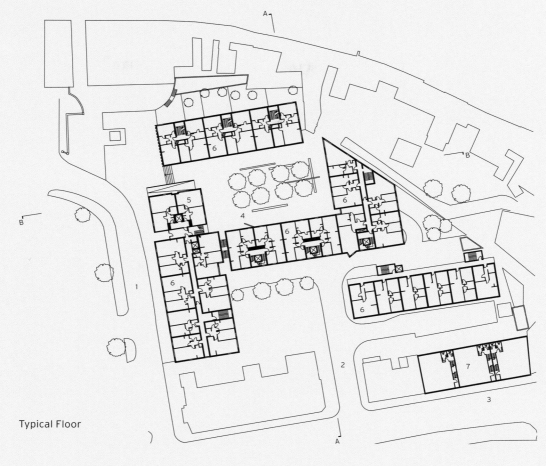

Typical Floor

GROUND FLOOR

1 Greyfriars Lane
2 Maidstone Road
3 Rose Lane
4 Courtyard
5 Tower
6 Residential
7 Commercial

Ground Floor

N

0 5 10   25

MEDICAL RESEARCH COUNCIL

SITE PLAN

1   New Extension
2   Edwardian Building
3   1960s Building
4   Chaucer Road
5   Gardens

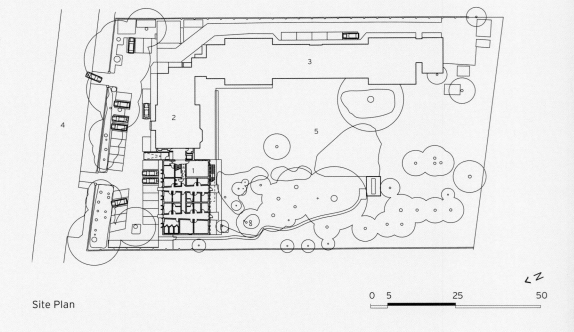

Site Plan

0   5   25   50

SECTIONS

1   Entrance
2   Link
3   Circulation
4   Lab
5   Lecture Theatre
6   Plant Room
7   Exterior Stair

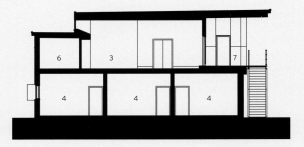

Section AA

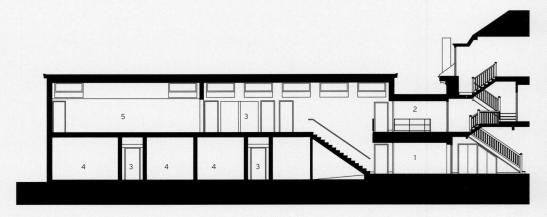

Section BB

FIRST FLOOR

1 Link
2 Circulation
3 Seminar Room
4 Lecture Theatre
5 Plant Room
6 Exterior Stair

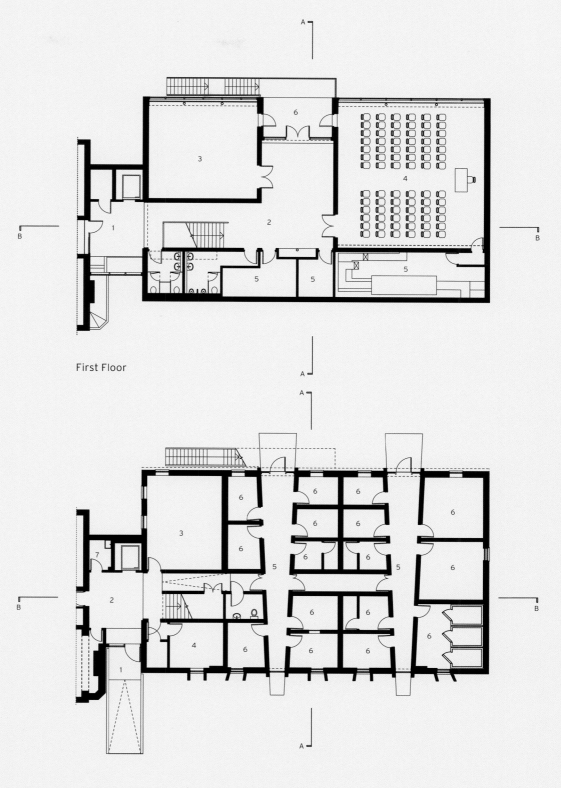

First Floor

GROUND FLOOR

1 Entrance
2 Link
3 Technical Department
4 Office
5 Circulation
6 Lab

Ground Floor

STONELEIGH ROAD

SITE PLAN

1 Stoneleigh Road
   Workspace Facility
2 Courtyard
3 Street Market
4 Stoneleigh Road
5 High Road
6 Brook Street

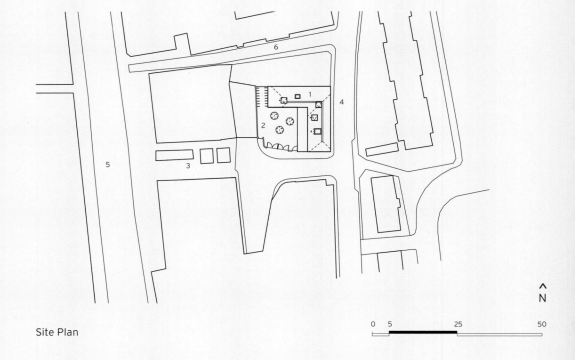

Site Plan

SECTIONS

1 Lobby
2 Office Space
3 Office/Meeting Room
4 Courtyard
5 Circulation

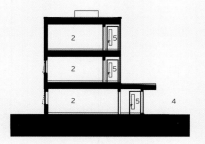

Section AA

Section BB

SECOND FLOOR

1   Lobby
2   Tea Room
3   Office Space
4   Office/Meeting Room
5   Vent Shafts

FIRST FLOOR

1   Lobby
2   Tea Room
3   Office Space
4   Office/Meeting Room
5   Vent Shafts

First Floor

Second Floor

GROUND FLOOR

1   Lobby
2   Post Room
3   Office Space
4   Bin Store
5   Office/Meeting Room
6   Vent Shafts
7   Courtyard

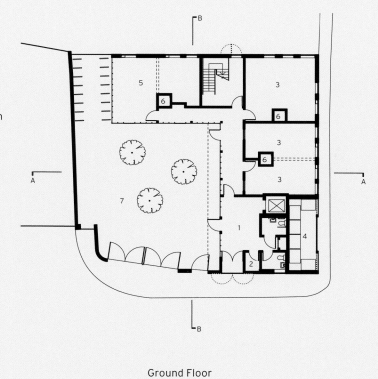

Ground Floor

N

0 1   5   10

SALVATION ARMY

SITE PLAN

1 Salvation Army Citadel
2 Courtyard
3 Baddow Road
4 Goldlay Road
5 Parkway Dual Carrigeway

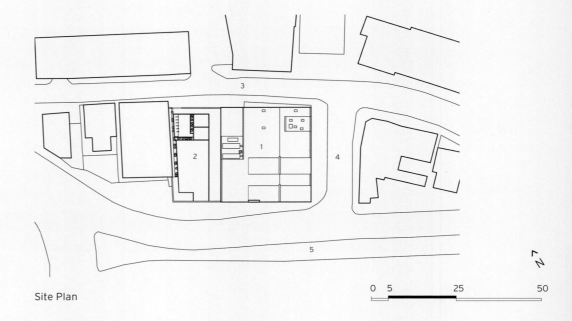

Site Plan

0 5   25   50

SECTIONS

1 Foyer
2 Toilet Lobby
3 Male WC
4 Worship Hall
5 Hall 2
6 Baby WC
7 Courtyard
8 Landing
9 Instrument Store

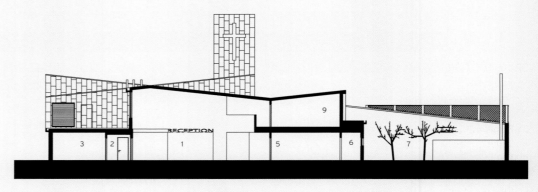

Section AA

Section BB

FIRST FLOOR

1 Commanding Officer
2 Admin Office
3 Instrument Store
4 Landing
5 Store
6 Plant Room
7 Plant Roof
8 Void

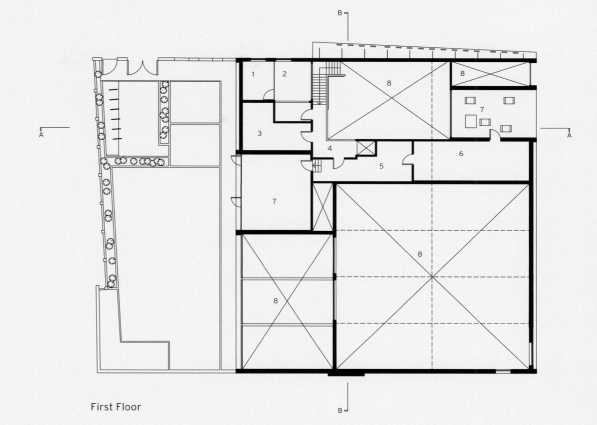

First Floor

GROUND FLOOR

1 Foyer
2 Multi-Purpose Room
3 Female WC
4 Toilet Lobby
5 Male WC
6 Disabled WC
7 Centre Manager
8 Lobby
9 Drop in Space/Cry Room
10 Worship Hall
11 WC
12 Baby Change
13 Cleaner
14 Lobby
15 Store
16 Lounge
17 Hall 2
18 Kitchen
19 Hall 1
20 Bin Store
21 Baby WC
22 Courtyard

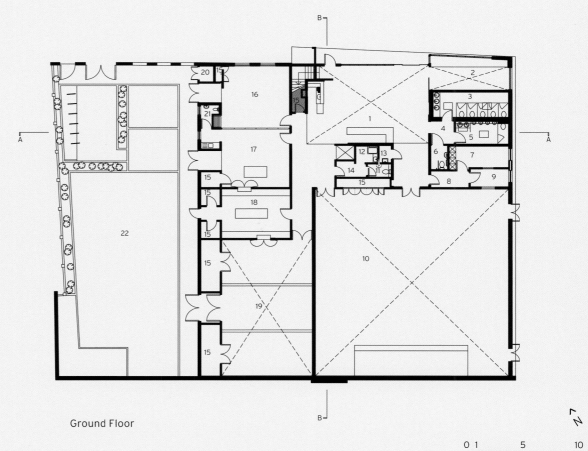

Ground Floor

0 1   5   10

ACKNOWLEDGEMENTS

Thanks to the following who have all contributed to the success of the practice past and present:

Leonora Aigbokae, David Appleton, Hannah Baker, Sophie Bates, Rebecca Behbahani, Robin Bertram, Richard de Boise, Matthew Bradbury, Sarah Bromley, Annabel Chown, Ross Coathup, Joanna Coleman, Kris Cowley, Alex Crossley, Janet Dunsmore, Philip Durban, Sarah Earney, Krista Evans, Sam Evans, Annie Farley-Kijowska, Sarah Featherstone, Sara Forbes-Jones, Lucy Furniss, Alexandra Gordon, Debbie Gray, Brian Greathead, Matt Griggs, Natalia Guerra, Oliver Hardisty, Ben Harriman, Naomi Hawkins-Day, Duncan Holmes, Mel Hosp, Wayne Head, Richard Hind, Anthony Hudson, Jeremy King, Dieter Kleiner, Thomas Kronig, Carlos Kucharek, Tina Lejon, Holly Lewis, Tom Lewith, Patrick Lovatt, Nicola Marsh, Jenny Martin, Ian McDonald, Lucy Minyo, Zac Monro, Jenn Moran, Evelyn Obiri, Rocio Pajuelo, Ruby Penny, Gareth Puttock, Rahesh Ram, Keith Reay, Ed Rhodes, Jana Rock, Suzanne Roles, Michelle Saywood, Amanda Spence, Daniel Swift-Gibbs, Jonathan Tipper, Bronwen Thomas, Richard Trew, Jeremy Walker, Nicole Weiner, Hannah Wooller, Angelika Zwingel.

A big thank you to all of our clients for their patronage and support over the years.

The essays by Jay Merrick, Peter Blundell Jones, Sarah Wigglesworth and Alan Power are much appreciated for their observations and insights.

Two buildings, Drop House and Medical Research Council, were undertaken under the practice name, Hudson Featherstone.

PHOTO CREDITS

Peter Blundell Jones, pp. 23 (centre).
James Brittain, pp. 13 (bottom), 17-19, 25 (third down, bottom), 26 (top), 58-61 (right), 62-67, 70 (centre), 71 (top), 72 (top, second down, third down), 82-88, 90, 91, 98-107.
Tim Brotherton, pp. 37-39, 47-51, 52 (top), 53, 132-135.
Michael Cameron, pp. 15 (bottom), 89.
Keith Collie, pp. 13 (top) 16, 26 (centre, bottom), 27 (bottom), 118-119 (centre, bottom), 120 (bottom), 121, 136-138, 139 (top, bottom), 146-155.
Roderick Coyne, pp. 22 (bottom), 23 (bottom) 24 (centre).
David Grandorge, pp. 46, 52 (bottom), 70 (top), 74-76 (right) 77-81.
Hudson Architects, pp. 22, 57 (top left, bottom right), 71 (centre, bottom).
Anthony Hudson, pp. 12, 33 (left), 57, 76 (left), 139 (centre).
Robin Hudson, p. 61 (left).
Country Life, pp. 29, 35 (top).
Mark Luscombe-Whyte, pp. 68.
James Mortimer, pp. 22 (top), 23 (top), 34 (right), 35 (bottom), 36 (right).
Cristobal Palma Photography, pp. 120 (centre), 140-145.
Jeremy Phillips, pp. 115 (top left, bottom left).
Richard Powers, pp. 92-97.
Jo Reid and John Peck, pp. 14, 20, 24 (top), 27, (top) 28, 30-33 (right), 34 (top left, bottom left), 36 (left).
Edmund Sumner, pp. 15 (top), 54-56, 57 (top right), 70 (bottom), 116, 119, 120 (top), 122-131.
Steve Townsend, pp. 10, 11, 15 (centre), 24 (bottom), 25 (top, second down), 40-45, 72 (bottom), 108-115 (right).

COLOPHON

© 2012 Artifice books on architecture, the architects and the authors.
All rights reserved.

Artifice books on architecture
10A Acton Street
London
WC1X 9NG

t. +44 (0)207 713 5097
f. +44 (0)207 713 8682
sales@artificebooksonline.com
www.artificebooksonline.com

All opinions expressed within this publication are those of the authors
and not necessarily of the publisher.

Designed by Mónica Oliveira at Artifice books on architecture.
Edited at Artifice books on architecture.

British Library Cataloguing-in-Publication Data.
A CIP record for this book is available from the British Library.

ISBN 978 1 908967 06 0

Artifice books on architecture is an environmentally responsible
company. An Open Mind is printed on sustainably sourced paper.